A Practical Guide
to
Algol 68

Frank G. Pagan
Memorial University of Newfoundland,
St. John's, Newfoundland,
Canada

A Wiley–Interscience Publication

JOHN WILEY & SONS
Chichester · New York · Brisbane · Toronto

Library of Congress Cataloging in Publication Data:

Pagan, Frank G.
   A practical guide to ALGOL 68.

   'A Wiley–Interscience publication.'
   Bibliography: p.
   Includes index.
   1. ALGOL (Computer program language) I. Title.
QA76.73.A24P34   001.6'424   75–6925

ISBN 0 471 65746 8 (Cloth)
ISBN 0 471 65747 6 (Pbk)

Photosetting by Thomson Press (India) Limited, New Delhi
and printed in Great Britain by The Pitman Press, Bath, Avon.

A Practical Guide
to
Algol 68

WILEY SERIES IN COMPUTING

Consulting Editor

C. A. Lang, Computer Laboratory, Cambridge University

Numerical Control—Mathematics and Applications

P. Bézier
Professeur au Conservatoire National des Arts et Métiers
and
Technological Development Manager, Renault, France

Communication Networks for Computers

D. W. Davies
and
D. L. A. Barber

National Physical Laboratory,
Teddington

**Macro Processors
and Techniques for Portable Software**

P. J. Brown
University of Kent at Canterbury

A Practical Guide to Algol 68

Frank G. Pagan
Memorial University of Newfoundland

Preface

The aims of this book are to provide an informal but comprehensive guide to the final (1974) version of the Algol 68 programming language and to do so in a manner consistent with the use of what has come to be known as structured programming. The book is intended to be useful to anyone wishing to gain a practical knowledge of the language, including those with no previous programming experience. It can therefore be used as a text for an introductory course in computer programming.

Algol 68 is a powerful and elegant language which was designed to serve both as a practical and efficient tool for a wide range of computer application areas and as a vehicle for the embodiment and development of many advanced concepts in the theory of programming languages. Although this book is primarily concerned with the first of these aspects, those with an academic interest in the language will be in a much better position to undertake a more theoretical study after having attained the level of skill which this book can provide. With this in view, I have used terminology which is largely consistent with that of the official language definition (see the bibliography), although not all of the technical terms used therein have been included. The treatment is independent of any particular machine or compiler, so that the book can be used in conjunction with any available implementation.

The structured approach to programming in a high-level language has become widely accepted, but only a very few texts to date have adopted it. Two of the major aspects of structured programming are 'top-down' program development and the disciplined use of control structures (loops, conditionals, routines, etc.). The former is largely beyond the scope of a book of this size because of the small scale of the examples and the need to concentrate on the language itself. With regard to the control structures of Algol 68, I have attempted to introduce them in such a manner as to develop systematically the basic techniques of writing correct and understandable programs. In particular, jump statements play only a minor role and are not used at all in most of the book.

The exposition generally moves from the particular to the general and from the simple to the more complicated. Some sections, whose headings are marked with an asterisk, describe elementary programming concepts and may be skipped by readers with experience in other programming languages. Whether they are beginners or not, readers who are interested in only one application area may not wish to master all aspects of the language and will not be interested in all the examples. Accordingly, sections which are marked with the letters SCO describe language features and examples related to symbolic or non-numeric processing and commercial applications, and may be skipped by those not interested in these aspects; sections marked NUM describe features and examples relevant only to numerical applications. Those who wish to learn the whole language should read all these sections. Each reader should attempt all the exercises in the sections he is reading; in addition, he should write and test other, preferably larger programs which either arise from his own interests or are suggested by his instructor. No exercises have been included in the last two chapters, as much of the material contained in them can be considered to be 'advanced' and supplementary to a basic knowledge of Algol 68. Appendix II contains a concise, semiformal summary of the syntax of the language.

Flowcharts do not appear at all in this book, as one of the features of structured programming is that the flow of control in a program should be clear from the program itself. Conventional flowcharts actually exert a negative influence, since they strongly suggest the possibility of constructing programs with an undisciplined and arbitrary structure. To those who believe that flowcharts nevertheless play an important role, I urge the adoption of some nonstandard scheme which is more consistent with good program structure, particularly with respect to the representation of loops.

F. G. PAGAN
April 1975

Contents

Chapter 1
Basic Concepts and Constructs

1.1 Computers and Programming*

This book describes a medium for the use of digital computers. Computers are used to perform tasks, such as complicated numerical calculations or the manipulation of large quantities of stored information, which can be rigorously defined but are too difficult or time-consuming to be done by hand.

The basic components of a typical digital computer system are shown schematically in Figure 1. The heart of the system is the CENTRAL PROCESSING UNIT or CENTRAL PROCESSOR, which consists of a CONTROL UNIT, an ARITHMETIC UNIT, and a MAIN STORE or MEMORY. There are also a number of PERIPHERAL DEVICES which serve to get information into and out of the memory of the central processor. Those which are used only for bringing information in, such as card readers and paper tape readers, are called INPUT peripherals. Those which are used only for getting information out, such as lineprinters, and paper tape punches, are called OUTPUT peripherals. Peripherals such as magnetic tape drives and disk drives, which may be

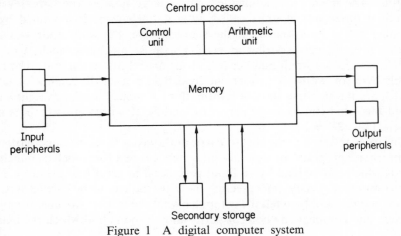

Figure 1 A digital computer system

used for both input and output, provide SECONDARY STORAGE or a BACKING STORE for the main memory. From a beginner's standpoint, only two peripherals are of any importance: one input device, typically a card reader, and one output device, normally a lineprinter.

It has been assumed so far that the type of service which the computer installation offers its users is that of BATCH PROCESSING. Under this mode of operation, the user typically submits to the operating staff a deck of punched cards which specify a JOB or unit of work which is to be carried out by the computer. Some time later, depending on how much work the computer has to cope with in relation to its capabilities, he receives back the cards and the lineprinter output from his job. An alternative type of service which an installation may offer in place of or in addition to batch processing is that of INTERACTIVE or ON-LINE PROCESSING. In this case, the user is concerned with only one peripheral device, such as a teletypewriter terminal, with which he can monitor or control the processing of his job. The interactive terminal is used for both input and output but differs from backing store devices in that information output to it is not stored for re-input at some later time.

Assuming a simple batch processing system, the card reader may be used to transfer the user's program and data for the program into the computer's memory. DATA is encoded information, such as numbers or alphabetic text, which is to be used or manipulated in some way. A PROGRAM is a set of instructions specifying how to input the data, what manipulations are to be carried out using the data, and what information is to be output as a result of these manipulations. Once the program is in the memory, the control unit, with the aid of the arithmetic unit, EXECUTES it; i.e., the various instructions for input, computation, and output are performed.

The memory contains not only the program, but also data which has been input, intermediate results during execution, and the results which are to be output. The memory is subdivided into a large number (perhaps several hundred thousand) of units called WORDS. Each word is identified by a number called its ADDRESS; in the simplest case, the word addresses are consecutive integers starting at zero. On most machines, each word is subdivided into a small number (e.g., four or six) of sections called BYTES. Each byte (or word) is further subdivided into a small number of BITS, which are the smallest units of information. A typical machine might have eight bits per byte, six bytes per word, and 512K words in its main store, where $1K = 2^{10} = 1024$.

In order to use a computer to carry out a given task, we must write an appropriate program for that task and encode it in a form such as punched cards which can be read by an input peripheral to get it into memory. The program must specify very precisely how the task is to be carried out. It is not enough simply to tell the computer what the task is; we must supply a precise and complete method for performing it, a method which the inanimate and unintelligent machine can follow surely and systematically to arrive at the desired results. Such a method is called an ALGORITHM. Programs may be thought of as one type of representation of algorithms. Algorithms can also be expressed in other ways, such as by flowcharts or by English descriptions. The essential difference between these and programs is that the latter are understandable to a computer.

As an example, suppose that we want the computer to determine whether a given number is prime. An algorithm for the solution of this problem might be roughly described as follows:

> First, divide the number by 2. If there is no remainder, divide it by 3, 4, etc. until either there is no remainder or the number itself is reached. In the former case, the number is not prime and in the latter case it is.

Now if this description were punched on cards and fed to a computer, nothing would be accomplished because the computer does not understand English. We must express the algorithm is a language which it does understand, and such a language is called a PROGRAMMING LANGUAGE. We must be familiar with a programming language in order to be able to write programs.

There are many different programming languages, and most computer systems understand more than one. A program in a computer's memory ready for execution is said to be expressed in the MACHINE LANGUAGE of the computer. This is the only language which the control unit directly understands but is very difficult for humans to understand and use. To avoid having to write our programs in machine language, we write them instead in a HIGH-LEVEL LANGUAGE and have the computer itself translate or COMPILE them into machine language. This is done using a specially provided program called a COMPILER which takes as input the program expressed in the high-level language (the SOURCE PROGRAM) and produces an equivalent machine language program (the OBJECT PROGRAM), which can then be executed. When a machine is provided with a compiler for a given high-level language, the language is said to be IMPLEMENTED on that machine.

High-level languages are relatively simple to learn and convenient to use. Algol 68 is a particularly powerful and convenient high-level language which is useful in a wide variety of application areas. Most other high-level languages are more specialized; Cobol, for example, is oriented towards commercial applications, and Algol 60 and Fortran were designed primarily for numerical calculations.

The entire process of preparing and using a simple Algol 68 program can be summarized in four steps:
1. Development of an algorithm
2. Coding in Algol 68
3. Compilation
4. Execution

The first step is often the most difficult. Even after we have found a algorithm to perform a certain task, it may turn out to be unacceptabl; inefficient; for example, the algorithm which was given for the prime numbei problem wastes considerable time on fruitless and unnecessary operations. Step 2 is relatively straightforward, provided that the programmer is thoroughly familiar with the language, and is often combined with step 1. After coding and punching, the program together with some test data can be submitted as a job to the computer system. At step 3 the compiler may detect some violations of the rules of the language and print out appropriate error messages or DIAGNOSTICS. In that case we must go back to step 2, correct the errors, and resubmit the job. When there are no compilation errors, the computer can execute the object program. Errors may also come to light at this stage when the execution does not proceed as expected, or does not give rise to the expected results. These 'logical' errors are often an indication that the algorithm is not completely correct, so that we must go back to step 1. This iterative process of removing the errors, or 'bugs', from a program is called DEBUGGING and is a normal part of program development. After a few runs, debugging should be complete and the program ready for practical use.

Algol 68 programs can be run on any computer system on which Algol 68 is implemented. The details of how to submit a job, informing the computer that it is an Algol 68 job, will vary from system to system. It is the business of constructing Algol 68 programs which is essentially machine independent and to which the remainder of this book is devoted.

Exercises

1. Re-express the given algorithm for determining whether a number is prime so that it is more efficient with respect to execution time.
2. Express in English an algorithm for calculating the average value of n numbers, given that only two numbers at a time may be added.

1.2 The Notation and Terminology of Algol 68

An Algol 68 source program is a hierarchically organized set of CONSTRUCTS specifying the actions to be carried out on various VALUES when the object program is executed. Each source program or constituent construct consists of a sequence of basic objects called SYMBOLS. A symbol as represented on paper may consist of a letter, a group of letters in boldface type, a digit, or some other character such as (or combination such as $:=$. (This definition is slightly different from the official one.) Thus there are 21 symbols in the following trivial program which inputs a single intege number and prints it out:

```
( int x;
  read (x);
  print (x) )
```

The single symbol **int** is an entirely different object from *int*, which consists of three symbols. Such boldface symbols are termed INDICANTS in this book, and there are many of them in Algol 68. In handwritten or typed programs, indicants are usually underlined. Some symbols are equivalent to each other; ↓ , for example, may be used in place of the indicant **down**. The presence of blank spaces or changes to a new line between symbols has no significance other than that of readability; very often each line of the printed program corresponds to one punched card. Single symbols, however, must not be split up by spaces or line boundaries.

Some symbol representations will have to be modified in order to be acceptable to a particular compiler or machine. If lower case letters are not permitted, for example, *int* might appear as INT and **int** as 'INT', where the only use in the language of the apostrophe character would be as a marker for indicants. These notational variations, or 'hardware representations', are of no further concern in this book. It is up to the programmer to ascertain and observe the particular ones in use at his installation.

There will also be variations of ENVIRONMENT from one implementation of the language to another. This term refers to such things as the maximum integer value which can be stored in the machine and certain language features whose exact definitions have been specifically left to the implementation. We shall see that there are facilities by which individual programs may take some of these variations into account.

A third kind of variation with which each programmer must concern himself arises from the fact that some implementations may be restricted to SUBLANGUAGES, where some features of the standard language have been omitted or extra restrictions imposed, and some may be extended to SUPERLANGUAGES, where additional features or interpretations have been included. In many cases both types of modification will have been made.

To facilitate the precise description of Algol 68 programs, the designers of the language introduced a considerable number of new technical terms. This may pose less of a problem for inexperienced beginners than for those with a knowledge of other languages. In the hope of reducing later confusion for readers in the latter group, a table of *approximate* correspondences between some of the Algol 68 terminology and the terminology of other languages is given below:

Algol 68	Other languages
assignation	assignment statement
closed clause	compound statement, block
coercion	type conversion
denotation	constant, literal
elaboration	execution, evaluation
formula	expression

Algol 68	Other languages
indicant	keyword
mode	data type
multiple value	array
name	location, variable
phrase	statement
range	block, scope
series	statement sequence
transput	input/output, I/O
unit	expression, statement

The ELABORATION of a construct is a more abstract concept than that of execution, since it may be thought of as the sequence of actions specified by that piece of Algol 68 text. There is often no need to consider the compilation process which produces an object program to be executed. We may wish to consider instead what would happen if the program text were executed directly on an 'Algol 68 machine'. This 'manual' or 'mental' elaboration is often more use to us conceptually than the 'real' elaboration which a computer carries out.

1.3 Denotations

1.3.1 Integers

A DENOTATION is a construct which represents some definite, fixed value belonging to a class of such values. For example, *15* is a denotation for the value fifteen, which belongs to the class of integer values. This denotation is then said to have the MODE **int**, which is one of several basic modes in the language. The denotation is a piece of program text; the value it represents, which is also said to have the mode **int**, acquires reality only by elaboration.

Any sequence of digits from *0* through *9* is a denotation of mode **int**. Some further examples follow:

    1000   *0*   *2541905*   *015*

Leading zeros are redundant, so that *015* represents the same value as *15*. No commas or decimal points are permitted in an integer denotation. The integer denotation with the smallest value is *0*; the largest value depends upon the environment but will in any case be finite.

1.3.2 Characters and Strings

A denotation of mode **char** consists of a letter, digit, or other character enclosed by quote symbols, as in

    "x"   *"5"*   *","*   *"+"*

The denotation for the quote character itself is $"""""$. The blank or space character is denoted by $"\_"$ or $"\quad"$; the latter is an exception to the rule that spaces have no significance in programs. The set of valid character denotations depends upon the environment. Note the distinction between $"5"$, a character denotation comparable to $"x"$ or $"+"$, and 5, an integer denotation comparable to 15 or 1000.

A denotation of mode **string** consists of any sequence (zero or two or more) of characters which can be contained in character denotations, enclosed by quote symbols. Some examples are

$$"a\_string\_denotation" \qquad "15" \qquad " " "algol\ 68" " "$$

There is again a distinction between $"15"$, which represents a string of two characters, and 15, which represents the integer value fifteen. The denotation $" "$ represents the NULL string or EMPTY string, which contains no characters at all. There is in principle no upper limit on the number of characters in a string.

1.3.3 Real Numbers

Unlike integers, numeric values of the mode **real** may have fractional parts, as indicated by the presence of decimal points within their denotations:

$$15.0 \qquad 5.747 \qquad .01 \qquad 03.14159$$

The decimal point cannot be the last symbol, so that 15. is not a valid real denotation.

Real numbers can also be written in FLOATING POINT form, where an integer or real denotation as described above is followed by an EXPONENT. The exponent part consists of the letter e, the symbol $_{10}$, or the symbol $\backslash$, optionally followed by one of the signs $+$ and $-$, followed by an integer denotation. The exponent specifies the number of places to the left or right that the decimal point is to be shifted. Thus the members of each of the following pairs of denotations are equivalent:

$$
\begin{array}{ll}
123.0 & 1.23e2 \\
123.0 & 123_{10} + 0 \\
.00023 & 2.3\backslash - 4
\end{array}
$$

If the exponent has no sign, it is assumed to be positive. The floating point notation is particularly convenient for denoting very large or very small real values. The largest and smallest (non-zero) real numbers and the largest number of significant figures in a single number all depend upon the environment.

Exercises

1. Which of the following are valid denotations of mode **int**?

     143   *1,000,000*   *00*   *5.4*   *3*   *"5"*

2. Which of the following are valid denotations of mode **string**?

     " "   *"a1b2c3"*   *" " "ab" "c"*   *" " "ab"c"*

How many characters are contained in the value represented by each of the valid ones?
3. Which of the following are valid denotations of mode **real**?

     012. $1_{10}1$ *63.123e–10*   *2.e3*   *47,101.6*

1.4 Variable Declarations

Denotations represent constant values which cannot be changed. One of the most fundamental aspects of programming is the use of NAMES, which can have different values at different times during the elaboration of a program. A name is said to REFER TO its value and is itself a value as opposed to a construct. In machine terms, a name is the location (i.e., address or addresses) containing the value to which it refers.

Names are represented in source programs by constructs called IDENTIFIERS, which will later be seen to have other uses as well; when an identifier represents a name, it is called a VARIABLE. An identifier is any sequence of one or more letters and digits where the first character must be a letter. No other characters are permitted. The following are examples of identifiers:

     a   *a1*   *average*   *x1y2z3*

The following are not valid identifiers:

     x(3)   *2b*   *a.b*   *number + 1*

Variables in general are used for names of values of all modes. A particular variable represents a name which ordinarily can refer only to values of a single mode which is specified in a VARIABLE DECLARATION such as

     int *n*

The symbol **int** in this context is called a DECLARER. The elaboration of the declaration involves the allocation of part (e.g., a word) of the machine's memory for the storage of an integer value; in other words, a new name for a value of mode **int** is created. This name, which is represented by the variable *n* in the source program, may later refer to different integer values at different times. Since the name itself is not an integer value but refers to one, it is said to have the mode **ref int**; i.e., it is a reference to an integer. The variable *n* is also said to have the mode **ref int**.

More than one variable of the same mode can be declared at the same time by listing them after the declarer and separating them by commas:

int *n1, n2, n3*

The three names are created in an unspecified order, so that, for example,

int *n3, n2, n1*

is an equivalent variable declaration.

Variables which refer (or, strictly speaking, which represent names which refer) to values of other modes are declared in an analogous way. For example,

real *x*

generates (when it is elaborated) a name of mode **ref real** represented by the variable *x*. The declarer in this case is the symbol **real**.

After the elaboration of

char *ch1, ch2*

ch1 and *ch2* will represent names of mode **ref char** which refer to values of mode **char**. Similarly,

string *s*

declares a variable *s* of mode **ref string** which refers to a string of zero or more characters. Since there is no definite limit to the amount of memory required for a string value, the allocation of storage during the elaboration of a string variable declaration presents some difficulty. Although this is a problem for the compiler implementer rather than the programmer, programs which use strings a great deal may be less efficient than other programs.

Exercises

1. Which of the following are valid identifiers?

   b2z   *2alpha*   *ttt*   *ab∗c*   *real*   **int**

2. Although the various identifiers used in a program are arbitrary as far as the computer is concerned, they are usually chosen so as to have some mnemonic significance for the programmer. Write declarations for two variables referring to the sum and the mean of some set of real numbers, and a variable referring to the number (an integer) of numbers in this set.

1.5 Operators and Simple Expressions

1.5.1 Numeric Formulas

Variable declarations as described in the preceding section do not provide the generated names with definite values to refer to. The ways in which names may be made to refer to other values will be discussed in the next chapter. For the present, we shall consider how values can be manipulated by the elaboration of FORMULAS in which their variables or denotations appear as OPERANDS.

1.5.1.1 Integer Arithmetic

Integer formulas are constructed with the aid of symbols for the common arithmetic operators. Some of these symbols are as follows:

+	addition
−	subtraction
* or ×	multiplication
↑ or ** or **up**	exponentiation

These operators are all DYADIC; i.e., they are applied to ordered pairs of operands which in this case have the mode **int**. When such a formula is elaborated, a new value of mode **int** is yielded. In the simplest case, both operands are denotations, as in the following examples:

$$15 + 537 \qquad 47 \uparrow 2 \qquad 4590 * 326$$

The values yielded by these formulas are *552, 2209,* and *1496340,* respectively.

Operations on denotations alone are not very useful, since we can always substitute denotations for the yielded values when we write the program in the first place. Many formulas contain variables as operands, as in

$$a + 1 \qquad 5 * b \qquad a - b$$

where a and b are assumed to have the mode **ref int**. In the formula $a + 1$, the intention is that the value 1 should be added to the value referred to by a;

the name itself does not take part in an addition. Thus the value referred to by a must be obtained before the addition can be carried out. This process is called DEREFERENCING, whereby in this case a value of mode **int** is obtained from a name of mode **ref int**. All names represented by variable operands in arithmetic formulas are dereferenced upon elaboration. Dereferencing is an example of a COERCION, an automatic process by which a value of one mode is obtained in a particular way from a value of another mode.

An operand in a formula may itself be a formula:

$$c * a + b \qquad b + c * a \qquad a + b + c + d$$

The order in which the operations are performed is partly determined by the PRIORITIES of the operators. Each dyadic operator has a priority between 1 and 9; $\uparrow$ has priority 8, $*$ has 7, and $+$ and $-$ have 6. It is the relative rather than the absolute values of the priorities that are important: operations of higher priority are performed first when necessary. Thus in the first two examples above, the multiplication of the values referred to by c and a is carried out first; the yielded value is then added to the value referred to by b. Successive operations of equal priority are carried out in left-to-right order, so that in the third example the values of a and b are added, yielding a value to which the value of c is added, yielding a value to which the value of d is added. In the case of

$$a * b + c * d$$

the multiplications are not ordered, but both must be carried out before the addition.

The (partial) ordering implied by these rules can be modified by the use of parentheses, as in the following formulas:

$$(b + c) * a \qquad ((a - b) * c) \uparrow 2$$

Here a subformula (operand) enclosed by a pair of parentheses is elaborated as before, but this elaboration must be completed before the yielded value can take part in another operation, even one of higher priority. Parenthesized subformulas can be nested to any depth as long as the parentheses are properly balanced; the innermost formulas must then be elaborated first. No harm is done by introducing parentheses unnecessarily, as in

$$(a \uparrow 2) * (b \uparrow 2)$$

where the exponentiations would be performed first anyway (but not in any particular order) since they have higher priority than multiplication.

There are two other dyadic operators which yield integer values from pairs of integer-valued operands. The operation of integer division, represented by $\div$, %, or **over**, yields the integral part of the result of dividing the left operand value by the right; there is no fractional part. Thus the values yielded by the formulas

$$3 \div 2 \qquad 11 \div 12$$

are *1* and *0*, respectively. The operator **mod**, also written as $\div *$, $\div \times$, %$*$, or % $\times$, yields the positive remainder from such a division, so that the formulas

$$3 \textbf{ mod } 2 \qquad 11 \textbf{ mod } 12$$

yield *1* and *11*, respectively. Both these operators have priority *7*, the same as multiplication.

As well as dyadic operators, which apply to pairs of operands, there are MONADIC operators which apply to single operands. The monadic operator $-$ permits the expression of negative integers such as -15; in general, it reverses the sign of the value to which it is applied. Although they are represented by the same symbol, the dyadic $-$ and the monadic $-$ are two distinct operators. There is also a monadic $+$ operator, which has no effect on the value of its operand but is sometimes useful for readability purposes. The operator **abs** yields the absolute value or modulus of the operand value. Thus all of the following formulas yield the value *15*:

$$\textbf{abs } 15 \qquad \textbf{abs} + 15 \qquad \textbf{abs} - 15 \qquad \textbf{abs} (-15)$$

(Note that whenever two or more monadic operators appear next to each other, the rightmost operation must be performed first.) The operator **sign** yields the value -1 if its integer operand is negative, *0* if it is zero, and $+1$ if it is positive.

All monadic operators have a higher priority (*10*) than any dyadic operator, so that, in formulas containing both types, parentheses must often be used in order to force a dyadic operation to be carried out before a monadic one. Thus the values yielded by the two formulas

$$-5 + 10 \qquad -(5 + 10)$$

are *5* and -15, respectively.

Exercises

1. What value is yielded by each of the following formulas?

(a) $3 + 20\%2 \uparrow 3$ (b) $5 * - \textbf{abs} (75 - 80 + 2)$
(c) $4 + - 2 \uparrow 2$

2. If *n1* refers to -5 and *n2* refers to *10*, what value is yielded by each of the following?

(a) $n2 - n1$ (b) $n1 * - n2 \div 2 * n2$
(c) $n1 * -n2 \div (2 * n2)$

1.5.1.2 Real Arithmetic

The operators for addition, subtraction, and multiplication as applied to pairs of real values to yield real values have the same symbols and priorities as those for integers. The symbol for division of real numbers is / and has priority 7. The monadic operators $-$, $+$, and **abs** are also analogous to the corresponding integer operators. Some examples of real formulas and their values are given below, where it is assumed that the variable x has the mode **ref real** and refers to the value *2.4*:

$x + 5.132e2$	yields	*515.6*
$1.2 - x/0.8$	yields	-1.8
$- x * -(x + 1.0)$	yields	*8.16*

1.5.1.3 Mixed Arithmetic

So far we have only considered operators which act upon values of a given mode and yield values of the same mode. There are also many operators where the modes occur in various mixtures, and this makes for considerable flexibility in writing arithmetic expressions.

There are operators for addition, subtraction, multiplication, and division (/) where one of the operands is integer-valued and the other is real-valued. The value yielded then has the mode **real** and is the value one would naturally expect from the operation:

$5 + 2.4$	yields	*7.4*
$2.4/5$	yields	*0.48*
$-2 * (12.6 - 1)$	yields	-23.2

When the operator / is applied to two integers, a real result is yielded; for example, *3/2* yields *1.5*. Real values can be raised to integral powers using the operator $\uparrow$, so that *2.4↑2* yields *5.76*.

There are some monadic operators which act upon values of one of the numeric modes and yield values of the other. When **sign** is applied to a real value, it yields an integer value of $+1$, 0, or -1. The operator **round** gives the nearest integer to the value of a real operand, and **entier**, also written as $\mathord{\llcorner}$, gives the largest integer which is less than or equal to the value of a real operand. Thus

sign -2.7	yields	-1
round 2.7	yields	3
round -2.7	yields	-3
entier 2.7	yields	2
entier -2.7	yields	-3
round -2.1	yields	-2
entier -2.1	yields	-3

All the operators introduced so far are summarized in the following table, which is the first of several to be found throughout this book. In addition to its symbol(s) and priority, each dyadic operator is characterized by a construction of the form

(ML, MR) MY

where ML and MR are the modes of the left and right operands, respectively, and MY is the mode yielded by the formula, i.e., the mode of the result. A monadic operator is indicated by a priority of 10 and a construction of the form

(MR) MY

The rationale for this notation will become apparent in Chapter 5.

Symbols	Priority	Modes
+	6	(int, int) int
		(real, real) real
		(real, int) real
		(int, real) real
+	10	(int) int
		(real) real
−	6	(int, int) int
		(real, real) real
		(real, int) real
		(int, real) real
−	10	(int) int

Symbols	Priority	Modes
		(real) real
* ×	7	**(int, int) int**
		(real, real) real
		(real, int) real
		(int, real) real
÷ % over	7	**(int, int) int**
/	7	**(real, real) real**
		(real, int) real
		(int, real) real
		(int, int) real
mod ÷* ÷× %* %×	7	**(int, int) int**
↑ ** **up**	8	**(int, int) int**
		(real, int) real
abs	10	**(int) int**
		(real) real
sign	10	**(int) int**
		(real) int
round	10	**(real) int**
entier	10	**(real) int**

Exercises

1. If *n* refers to the integer 5 and *x* refers to the real number 2.6, what mode and value are yielded by each of the following formulas?

   (a) $n \div 2$ (b) $n/2$
   (c) $n * x$ (d) **entier** $(n/2)$
   (e) **round** $(n / 2)$ (f) $x / 2 * n$
   (g) $x / (2 * n)$ (h) $x \uparrow 2$

1.5.2 Non-numeric Expressions (SCO)

We turn now to operations which are used in the manipulation of character and string values. Two strings can be concatenated using the operator + to yield a longer string:

   "ab + "cde"   yields   "abcde"
   "no." + " " "9" " "   yields   "no." "9" " "

If the value of one of the operands is the empty string, the value yielded is that of the other operand:

   "ab" + " "   yields   "ab"

Concatenation is also defined when the value of one or both of the operands is a character:

$$"a" + "bcd" \qquad \text{yields} \qquad "abcd"$$
$$"a" + "b" \qquad \text{yields} \qquad "ab"$$

A character or string can be 'multiplied' by an integer value N to yield a string consisting of N copies of the original string concatenated together. As examples, all of the following formulas yield the value $"aaaaaa"$:

$$6 * "a" \qquad "a" * 6$$
$$3 * "aa" \qquad "aa" * 3$$
$$2 * "aaa" \qquad "aaa" * 2$$

A facility known as TRIMMING may be used to extract substrings from longer strings: a string variable may be followed by a pair of integer expressions (e.g., denotations, variables, or formulas) enclosed by square brackets or parentheses and separated by a colon. The integer expressions specify the position numbers in the string of the first and last characters of the yielded string. For example, if s refers to the string $"abcdef"$, and n refers to the integer 5, then

$$s[1:3] \qquad \text{refers to} \qquad "abc"$$
$$s[n-1:n] \qquad \text{refers to} \qquad "de"$$

The mode of each of these expressions is **ref string**. If the substring is to consist of only one character, we may use a single integer expression, which is then called a SUBSCRIPT:

$$s[3] \qquad \text{refers to} \qquad "c"$$

The mode of $s[3]$ is **ref char**. None of these expressions is a formula in the strict sense; their true nature will become apparent in Chapter 3.

For the type of string considered so far, the value of a subscript must not exceed the length (number of characters) of the string. The length can be determined using the monadic operator **upb** or Γ. One use of **upb** would be the extraction of the final character in a string of unspecified length:

$$s[\textbf{upb}\ s] \qquad \text{refers to} \qquad "f"$$

In a non-numeric expression, trimming takes precedence over the action of an operator. Thus

$$"xy" + s[3:5] \qquad \text{yields} \qquad "xycde"$$

$("xy" + s) [3:5]$ yields $"abc"$
$s[$**upb** $s - 1] * 3$ yields $"eee"$

There is a monadic operator **abs** which applies to operands of mode **char** and yields a unique integer value for each permissible character value. The actual correspondence between characters and integers depends upon the environment, but it will frequently be such that the values corresponding to the letters $"a"$ through $"z"$ and those corresponding to the digits $"0"$ through $"9"$ are consecutive and ascending. The monadic operator **repr** is the inverse of **abs**; i.e., when applied to an integer operand, it yields the corresponding character. All the operators which have been introduced in this section are summarized below:

Symbols	Priority	Modes
+	6	(string, string) string
		(string, char) string
		(char, string) string
		(char, char) string
* ×	7	(string, int) string
		(int, string) string
		(char, int) string
		(int, char) string
upb (	10	(string) int
abs	10	(char) int
repr	10	(int) char

Exercises

1. If x refers to $"abcdef"$, what mode and value are yielded by each of the following?

(a) $x[2:5] + " "$ (b) **repr abs** $"*"$
(c) $5 +$ **upb** x (d) $x + x[6]$
(e) $x[3:4] + x[4:5] * 3$

Chapter 2
Straight-line Programs

2.1 Assignment

An ASSIGNATION is a construct which specifies that a given name is to be made to refer to the value yielded by a given expression. In the simplest case, it has the form

variable := expression

where the expression can be, for example, a denotation, variable, or formula. The mode of the value yielded by the expression must be appropriate to the name yielded by the left side; for example, if the name has the mode **ref int**, then the expression must yield a value of mode **int** (but see below). Elaborating the assignation has the effect that the value currently referred to by the name is replaced by the value yielded by the expression; the latter value is said to be ASSIGNED to the name. The symbol := (pronounced 'becomes') is not an operator in the strict sense, and assignment takes place only after all operations specified in the expression to its right have been performed.

2.1.1 Assignment of Numeric Values

If i and j are of mode **ref int** and j currently refers to the value *15*, then the elaboration of

$$i := j + 5$$

causes i to refer to the value *20*. Unlike j, i is not dereferenced; the value that it referred to prior to the assignment is irrelevant.

When the left side of an assignation yields a name of some mode **ref M**, the right side is required to yield a value of mode M. If M is **real**, however, the right side may be an integer expression; the integer value will be automatically converted to the corresponding real value and assigned to the real name. This coercion from **int** to **real** is called WIDENING. In the assignation

$$p := 5$$

the new value of p, which is assumed to have the mode **ref real**, is the real number 5.0, which is obtained by widening the integer 5. On the other hand, there is no coercion from **real** to **int**, so that

$$i := p$$

is incorrect and should be replaced by one of

$$i := \textbf{entier } p$$
$$i := \textbf{round } p$$

depending on the type of conversion desired.

An assignation as a whole yields a value which is the name yielded by its left side. It can therefore be used as the expression on the right side of another assignation. Thus in

$$i := j := 5$$

the value assigned to i is obtained from the value yielded by $j := 5$. Since this value is the name represented by j, it must be dereferenced to yield the value 5 which has just been assigned to it. Both names are thus assigned the value 5. In this way, any number of names can be assigned the same value. After the elaboration of

$$p := i := j := 5$$

for example, the respective values of i, j, and p will be 5, 5, and 5.0; two coercions of dereferencing and one of widening will be involved in carrying out the three assignments.

When an assignation is used as an operand in a formula, it must be parenthesized. Thus

$$4 + i := 5$$

is invalid for the standard meanings of $+$, but the valid formula

$$4 + (i := 5)$$

involves dereferencing i after the assignment and yields 9.

In the case of

$$i := i + 1$$

i is not dereferenced on the left side but on the right it is, so that the new value of *i* depends on its previous value (the value is increased by *1*). Since assignments of this type are very common, the language provides some arithmetic operators, called ASSIGNING OPERATORS, which carry them out automatically. The dyadic operator **plusab** ('plus and becomes') or $+:=$, for example, specifies that the numeric values yielded by its operands are to be added and the result assigned to the left operand, which must yield a name. Thus the formula

   x **plusab** *y*

has the same effect as the assignation

   $x := x + y$

Similarly, we have the following pairs of equivalent constructs:

x **minusab** *y*	$x := x - y$
x **timesab** *y*	$x := x * y$
x **overab** *y*	$x := x \div y$
x **modab** *y*	$x := x \bmod y$
x **divab** *y*	$x := x / y$

The operands may occur in the mode mixtures shown in the following table:

Symbols			Priority	Modes
plusab	$+:=$		*1*	(ref int, int) ref int
				(ref real, real) ref real
				(ref real, int) ref real
minusab	$-:=$		*1*	(ref int, int) ref int
				(ref real, real) ref real
				(ref real, int) ref real
timesab	$*:=$	$\times:=$	*1*	(ref int, int) ref int
				(ref real, real) ref real
				(ref real, int) ref real
overab	$\div:=$	$\%:=$	*1*	(ref int, int) ref int
modab	$\div*:=$	$\div\times:=$	*1*	(ref int, int) ref int
	$\%*:=$	$\%\times:=$		
divab	$/:=$		*1*	(ref real, real) ref real
				(ref real, int) ref real

In a formula containing any of these new operators, the yielded value is the name given by the left operand. Thus we have the following equivalences:

$$i := j \textbf{ plusab } 1 \qquad i := j := j + 1$$
$$p \textbf{ timesab } q + 5 \qquad p := p * (q + 5)$$

Note that the priority (1) of all the assigning operators is lower than that of any other operator. This means, for example, that

$$5 + q \textbf{ timesab } p$$

is erroneous for the standard meanings of $+$, since the left operand of **timesab** does not yield a name.

Exercises

1. If the current values of i, j, x, and y are $2, 3, 1.5$, and 2.4, respectively, for each of the following constructs list the variables whose values will be replaced together with their new values:

   (a) $i := j + 5$
   (b) $x := j + 5$
   (c) $y := j := i := \textbf{entier } (x * y)$
   (d) $i \textbf{ modab } j + 2$
   (e) $x := y \textbf{ timesab } i$

2. In each of the above, list all coercions, arithmetic operations, and assignments which will be carried out during elaboration. For example, the steps in elaborating (a) are as follows:

   Dereferencing j
   addition
   Assignment to i

3. If the modes of the variables are the same as in question 1, what is wrong with each of the following constructs?

   (a) $i := x + 1$ (b) $i := \textbf{entier } x := y - 2$
   (c) $i \textbf{ minusab } x$ (d) $x - y \textbf{ divab } 3$
   (e) $2 \textbf{ plusab } i$

4. Rewrite the following assignations using assigning operators:

   (a) $j := j - 1$ (b) $x := y * x$

(c) $i := i + i + 1$ (d) $y := x * y * 5$
(e) $x := y := y / j$

2.1.2 Assignment of Non-numeric Values (SCO)

Suppose that $c1$ and $c2$ are of mode **ref char**, $s1$ and $s2$ are of mode **ref string**, and i and j are of mode **ref int**. Then all of the following are straightforward examples of assignations involving non-numeric expressions:

$c1 := "a"$
$c2 := $ **repr** 16
$s1 := c2 + j * "xyz"$
$s2 := s1[1:j] + $ **repr** i
$i := $ **abs** $"*" * (j + $ **upb** $s1)$

In each case the mode of the variable on the left side is a reference to the mode of the value yielded by the right side.

It is also possible to assign a character value to a string name, as in

$s1 := c1$
$s2 := """"$

The coercion which in this case converts a value of mode **char** to the corresponding value of mode **string** is called ROWING. Its role here is clearly analogous to that of widening in the case of arithmetic assignment. There is no coercion from **string** to **char**, even if the current length of the string is 1. However, it is possible to write an assignation such as

$c1 := s1[1]$

since subscripting a name of mode **ref string** yields a name of mode **ref char**, which can be dereferenced to yield a character value.

In the examples so far of assignment to string names, the current value is replaced by a completely different string, possibly with a different length. By subscripting or trimming the variable on the left side, it is also possible to change only some of the characters in the current value, leaving the length unchanged. For example, if $s1$ currently refers to $"abcd"$, then

$s1[3] := "x"$

will change its value to $"abxd"$, while

$s1[2:4] := "xyz"$

will change it to $"axyz"$. The right side must yield a character or string value of a length equal to the number of characters to be replaced. The value on the right side may be taken from the same string, so that

$$s1[1:3] := s1[2:4]$$

will change the value of $s1$ from *"abcd"* to *"bcdd"*.

As with numeric assignations, a value can be assigned to more than one name:

$$s1 := s2 := "abc"$$
$$s1 := c2 := c1 := s2[\textbf{upb } s2]$$

In the case of

$$c1 := s1[i] := "a"$$

the value yielded by the right assignation is the name represented by $s1[i]$ of mode **ref char**. This is then dereferenced to yield *"a"*, which is assigned to $c1$. In the case of

$$s2 := s1[1:3] := s1[2:4]$$

the right assignation changes some of the characters in $s1$ as before and yields the name $(s1[1:3])$ of a string of length 3 which is assigned to $s2$.

The assignation

$$s1 := s1 + s2$$

which has the effect of concatenating some characters to the right end of $s1$, can be replaced by the formula

$$s1 \textbf{ plusab } s2$$

Similarly,

$$s1 := s2 + s1$$

which has the effect of concatenating some characters to the left end of $s1$, can be replaced by

$$s2 \textbf{ plusto } s1$$

Finally,

$$s1 := s1 * 5$$

can be replaced by

s1 **timesab** *5*

These assigning operators are summarized in the following table:

Symbols		Priority	Modes
plusab $+:=$		*1*	**(ref string, string) ref string**
			(ref string, char) ref string
plusto $+:=$		*1*	**(string, ref string) ref string**
			(char, ref string) ref string
timesab $*:=$ $\times:=$		*1*	**(ref string, int) ref string**

Exercises

1. If the current values of *s1* (**ref string**), *s2* (**ref string**),*c1* (**ref char**), and *i* (**ref int**) are *"abcd"*, *"pqrst"*, *"5"*, and *24*, respectively, for each of the following constructs list the variables whose values will be changed together with their new values:

    (a) $s1 := c1 + s2$
    (b) $s1 := "a"$
    (c) $s1 := c1 :=$ **repr** *i*
    (d) $s1[1:3] := s2[3,i - 19] := s1[2:4]$
    (e) *c1* **plusto** *s1*
    (f) $s1 := s2$ **plusab** $s2[1:4]$

2. Point out the errors in each of the following constructs, where the modes and current values are the same as in question 1.

    (a) $i :=$ **repr** *i*   (b) $c1 := s1 := "a"$
    (c) $s1[2:4] := s2 * 3$ (d) $s1[2:4]$ **plusab** *c1*
    (e) *s1* **plusto** *"ab"*

2.2 Simple Forms of Transput

The term TRANSPUT covers all processes by which information is obtained from or delivered to peripheral devices under the control of an Algol 68 program. In this section we restrict our attention to simple operations involving a standard input peripheral and a standard output peripheral. These standard devices may vary from one installation to another but frequently consist of a card reader and a lineprinter.

2.2.1 Input

Input operations constitute a second means by which names can acquire values during the elaboration of a program. If the value of a variable n is to be obtained from the data supplied with the program, we may write

> *read* (n)

This will cause the current value, if any, of n to be replaced by a new value in much the same way as in an assignation, except that the value is obtained from outside the program. The construct is an example of a CALL, where *read* is the identifier of a predefined PROCEDURE and n is an ACTUAL PARA-METER. These terms will be fully explained in Chapter 5; for the present, the reader is merely advised not to attempt to use the procedure identifiers introduced in this chapter for any other than the stated purposes.

The actual parameter of *read* must have one of the **ref** modes, such as **ref int** or **ref real**. The call as a whole does not yield any value; consequently, it is said to have the mode **void**, for which there are no values at all. Values for more than one name can be input by making the actual parameter a parenthesized list of variables separated by commas, as in

> *read* $(\,(n, x, i, abc)\,)$

The variables in the list may have different modes. The data supplied with the program should be thought of as a stream of characters divided into lines (e.g., cards). At any given time the program will have input all the values up to a certain position in the stream; this position in the simplest case moves in a forward direction. Numeric values in the data are separated by spaces and line boundaries. Elaboration of the above call would cause the next four values starting from the current position to be assigned in order to the four names and the current position to be updated.

In the case of integer and real values, the first group of nonblank characters to be found past the current position in the data must be recognizable as a value of the relevant mode. The value must be expressed within a single line in much the same way as a denotation which includes no intervening spaces, except that it may be preceded by a sign ($+$ or $-$) and possibly some spaces. The sign, if any, in an exponent part may also be preceded or followed by spaces. Furthermore, a value expressed as an integer is accept-able as a real number. As an example, suppose that i and j are integer vari-ables and x, y, and z are real variables. Then when

> *read* $(\,(x, y, i, j, z)\,)$

is elaborated, the next five values in the data stream might appear as follows:

$$- 12.34e - 2 \qquad 902$$
$$+14 \qquad 75 \qquad 345\backslash12$$

The arrangement of the values on different lines is irrelevant. If there are insufficient values left in the data, an error will occur; the user of the program should therefore ensure that this situation will not arise.

2.2.2 Output

The value yielded by any expression of the types considered so far can be output by making the expression an actual parameter in a call of one of the equivalent procedures *print* and *write*, as in the following examples:

> *print* (x)
> *write* (5)
> *write* $("result")$
> *print* $(a * (b + 2) + $ **sign** $p)$

The output data stream is divided into lines and pages; for a lineprinter, there might be 120 characters per line and 60 lines per page. Values of the modes **int** and **real** are printed beginning at the current position in the stream and are preceded by a space except at the beginning of a line. A new line is begun automatically whenever there is insufficient room for the value on the current line, and a new page is begun whenever there is insufficient room on the current page. All numeric values are immediately preceded by a sign. Real values are expressed in floating point notation with the maximum number of significant digits and one non-zero digit before the decimal point, and integers are preceded by a number of spaces so as to take up the same number of positions as the maximum integer value.

A call of *print* or *write* may output more than one value, as in

> *print* $((x, 5, "result", a * (b + 2) + $ **sign** $p))$

The values yielded by the expressions are output in order as described above. The layout of the output can be modified by including the identifiers *newline* and *newpage* within the actual parameter of *print*; *newline* causes immediate termination of the current line, and *newpage* causes immediate termination of the current page. In addition, the identifier *space* causes one output position to be skipped, while *backspace* causes the current position to be moved back by one character, but never past the beginning of the current line.

A character or string value is printed with no preceding space and without enclosing quotes. In the case of a string, its characters are printed one by one;

if it will not fit on the remainder of the current line, it is continued on the next line. Strings are particularly useful as headings and explanatory comments within the printout.

To illustrate some of these points, here are some examples of output constructs and the resulting portion of the printout, assuming in each case that the current output position is at the beginning of a line:

(a) *print* ((*newpage, "values", 12.3, 24*))

might produce (depending on the maximum real and integer values)

```
values +1.23000e +1       +24
```

at the top of a page.

(b) *print* ((*"heading", newline, −456, newline, 0, newline, 1000*))

might produce

```
heading
 −456
 +0
+1000
```

(c) *print* ((*−3.4, space, "a", 2.1e14, space, "b"*))

might produce

```
−3.40000e +0 a +2.10000e+14 b
```

The standard output format for an integer or real value can be modified by replacing the expression in the *print* call by a call of one of the procedures *whole*, *fixed*, and *float*, with the expression as the first actual parameter. In each case, the second parameter yields an integer specifying the width (total number of characters) of the printed string representing the value; if this number is positive, a sign is always printed, and if it is negative, a sign is printed only if the value is negative. If the width is insufficient for the string form of the value, the printed string is filled with characters given by the predefined identifier *error char* (see 2.3.3). If the width is 0, however, the value is printed in the minimum amount of space, with no leading spaces or + sign.

The procedure *whole* converts an integer (or a real number which it rounds to an integer) into a string. Thus, if *error char* is "?",

print (*(whole (9999, − 4), whole (99,5), whole (0,–3),*
     whole (–99,0), whole(9999,3), whole(9.3,–3)))

will produce the output

9999   +99   0–99???   9

The procedure *fixed* converts an integer or real number into a string representation which includes a decimal point followed by a number of digits given by a third parameter. If the parameter values are such that the width is not large enough but can be made so by reducing the number of digits following the point, the conversion will still succeed. As an example,

print (*(fixed(2,5, 2), space, fixed(2, − 5,1),*
     space, fixed(2.72,0,2), space,
     fixed(271.828,−6,3), space, fixed(271.828,0,3),
     space, fixed(99999,4,3)))

will produce the output

+2.00   2.0 2.72 271.83 271.828 ?????

The procedure *float* converts an integer or real number into a string representing the number in floating point notation with one non-zero digit before the decimal point. The first three parameters are like those of *fixed*, and a fourth specifies the width of the exponent, including its sign. Thus

print (*(float(− 2.718,9,3,2), space,*
     float(0.2718,9,3,2), space,
     float(2.718e11,9,3,2)))

will produce

−2.718e+0 +2.718e−1 +2.72e+11

2.3 Writing Simple Programs

2.3.1 Basic Program Structure

We now have enough basic tools for the composition of simple but complete programs. First we define some more technical terms.

A STATEMENT is a construct which has the mode **void** or which yields some value which is not immediately used. In the latter case, the value is said to undergo the coercion of VOIDING, whereby it is simply discarded. This often happens with assignations, where no use is made (at least for the time being) of the yielded name. Procedure calls yielding **void** are another kind of statement. Thus the following constructs are all simple examples of statements:

$$a := d + e \uparrow 2$$
$$print\ (\ (newline, x * y)\ )$$
$$x := y := z$$

In the last example, the assignation $y := z$ is not a statement since some use is made of its value y: it is dereferenced and the resulting value is assigned to x. The assignation is thus being used as an EXPRESSION, which we now define as any construct yielding a value which immediately takes part in some further operation. Similarly, in

$$print\ (x := 5)$$

$x := 5$ is an expression; 5 is output following an assignment and a dereferencing.

A UNIT (also called a UNITARY CLAUSE in some publications) is any construct which is either a statement or an expression. A PHRASE is any construct which is either a declaration (e.g., a variable declaration) or a unit. An Algol 68 source program usually consists of a sequence of phrases separated (as opposed to terminated) by semicolons and enclosed either by parentheses or by the symbols **begin** and **end**. When a given phrase is elaborated, a following semicolon is an indication to go on to the next phrase; consequently, no semicolon may follow the last phrase. The following construct is an example of a program:

```
begin int x, y, z;
    read ( (x, y) );
    z := x + y;
    print ( (x, y, z, 2 * z) ) end
```

This is a 'straight-line' program in the sense that the phrases will be elaborated in the sequence shown, and each will be elaborated exactly once.

Each identifier used in the units of such a straight-line program must be declared once and only once, except for predefined identifiers such as *read* and *print*. The declaration of an identifier must be elaborated before all units containing it, and the last phrase in the program must be a unit.

Elaboration of the above program proceeds phrase by phrase as follows:
(1) three names of mode **ref int**, represented by the variables x, y, and z,

are created; (2) two integer values are input so that they are referred to by *x* and *y*; (3) the values of *x* and *y* are added and the result assigned to *z*, which is voided; (4) the values of *x*, *y*, *z*, and $2 * z$ are printed in order.

As well as phrases, which cause various things to happen during elaboration, a program may contain COMMENTS, which do not affect the elaboration but serve only to make the program more understandable to the human reader. A comment is enclosed by a matching pair of one of the symbols **comment**, **co**, #, and ¢. The comment may be of any length and may contain any characters or sequences of characters whatsoever except the delimiting comment symbol (which terminates it). It may be inserted before any symbol in a program except within denotations or identifiers. The following program contains several comments:

> **comment** example of a program with comments **comment**
> (**int** *a*   **co** first operand **co**,
>   *b*   # second operand # ;
>   *read* ((*a, b*));   ¢ # input the operand values, # ¢
>   *print* (*a* * *b*)   ¢# and print the product #¢)

A PRAGMAT is superficially similar to a comment and is delimited either by two **pragmat** or by two **pr** symbols. The text which may appear within a pragmat is defined only by the implementation, and the information conveyed is not determined by the language proper. For example,

> **pragmat** *compile only* **pragmat**

might specify that the program is not to be executed after being compiled, and

> **pr finish pr**

might mark the end of the source program.

Exercises

1. For each of the following straight-line programs, classify each phrase as either a declaration or a unit, and briefly describe the elaboration of the program phrase by phrase.

   (a) (**int** *a, b*;
          read ((*a, b*));   ¢ input two integers,   ¢
          print((*a* + *b*,   ¢ print their sum,   ¢
             a * *b*,   ¢ product,   ¢

$a \div b$))   ¢ and integer quotient ¢)

(b) (**int** x, y, z; *read* ((x, y, z));
    real *avg*; *avg* := ($x + y + z$) / 3;
    print ((*avg*, **abs** (*avg* − x), **abs** (*avg* − y), **abs** (*avg* − z))))

2. Point out the errors in the following programs:

(a) (**int** i; *read* (i); *print*(i); **int** i; *read*(i); *print*(i))
(b) (*read*(i); **int** i, j; *read*(j); *print*((i, j)))
(c) (**int** i; *read*(i); *print*(i); **int** j)
(d) ($\# -- \# -- \# -- \#$ *print*("abcd"))
(e) (**int** i; *read*(j); *print*(j))

2.3.2 The Design and Testing of Simple Programs*

Many simple programs consist essentially of statements to input some values, followed by some statements to manipulate these values and assign the results to names, followed by statements to print out the results. Suppose we want to write a program to find and print the sum of the squares of the two integers *323* and *196*. The first point is that the program should be reasonably general; i.e., it should work for any two integers and not just these two. This makes the program much more useful since it may then be run many different times with different data; otherwise, it would be a 'one-shot' program which produced only one possible result. Indeed, it would not be worth the trouble to use a computer at all for such a simple once-only calculation. To input two values, then, we may use the statements

    read (i); *read* (j)

or, more simply and more efficiently,

    read ((i, j))

To do the required calculation and save the result as the value of a variable r, we may write

    $r := i * i + j * j$

The result can be printed using

    print (r)

We now see that we have used three variables i, j, and r, which will all have integer values, so that they can be declared as

> **int** i, j, r

The complete program may therefore be written as

> (**int** i, j, r; $read\ ((i, j))$;
> $r := i * i + j * j$;
> $print\ (r)$)

This program is more complicated than necessary. If we put the sum-of-squares formula directly in the output statement, we can dispense with r and the assignation:

> (**int** i, j; $read\ ((i, j))$;
> $print\ (i * i + j * j)$)

Now suppose that we also want to print the number which is double the result. We could modify the program as follows:

> (**int** i, j; $read\ ((i, j))$;
> $print\ ((i * i + j * j,$
> $2 * (i * i + j * j)))$)

This is inefficient because the same sum-of-squares calculation is performed twice. Now it is better to use an additional variable:

> (**int** i, j, r; $read\ ((i, j))$;
> $r := i * i + j * j$;
> $print\ ((r, 2 * r))$)

Once a program is written, it should be tested by running it with data for which the expected output values are known. We might test the above program with the data values *3* and *4* to make sure that it prints *25* and *50* as the results. If the results are incorrect, or if some execution error occurs so that no results at all are obtained, we may be able to find the bug by inspection of the program. If that fails, we can insert output statements at various points to determine the values of variables at different times. For example, if the data has been punched incorrectly, this might be detected by printing the values of i and j just after the input operation. Once the error is corrected, the program is retested for more errors. When the program has been tested enough to be considered correct, it may be used with the realistic data. Of course it is unlikely that these techniques will be necessary for programs as simple as those considered so far. Also, preventing bugs is usually less trouble than curing them, and considerable care should be taken to produce a program which is relatively free of errors by the time it is first run.

The use within an expression of a variable which has not been given a value in any previous phrase is a common pitfall. The following program, for example, will cause trouble when it is executed:

(**int** *i*; *i* **plusab** *1*; *print* (*i*))

Whenever a name is dereferenced, it should refer to some meaningful value which it has acquired, for example, by the elaboration of an assignation or an input statement. A third possibility is described in the following section.

Exercises

1. Write a compact program to input five integers and output their average value.
2. Write an efficient program which inputs integer values for *i* and *j* and outputs the values of i^2, j^2, i^2, $+ j^2$ and $i^2 - j^2$.

2.3.3. Initialization and Identity Declarations

A name can be assigned an initial value within its variable declaration. For example, the initializing variable declaration

int *i* := *15*

is equivalent to the pair of phrases

int *i*; *i* := *15*

Subsequently, of course, *i* may be assigned different values.

Any expression may appear to the right of :=, as long as it yields a value of the required mode (**int** in this case). All the coercions and evaluation rules which apply to assignations also apply to initializing declarations. Consider, for example, the following sequence:

int *a* := *5*;
int *b*;
b := *a* * *a*;
int *c* := *a* * (*b* + *5*)

Each variable is declared and given a value before it is used. The calculation of the initial value (*150*) of *c* involves dereferencing *a* and *b*, which got their respective values in an initializing declaration and an assignation. The second and third phrases could be replaced by another initializing declaration. Another possibility would be the use of

> *read* (*b*)

in place of the third phrase.

Initializing and non-initializing variable declarations can be combined in the same phrase, as in

> **int** *a*, *b* := *15*, *c* := *0*, *d*

However, since the order of elaboration of the parts separated by commas is undefined, an expression for an initial value should not contain a variable which is initialized in the same phrase, as in

> **int** *a*, *b* := *15*, *c* := *b* + *5*

This should be replaced by

> **int** *a*, *b* := *15*; **int** *c* := *b* + *5*

An IDENTITY DECLARATION specifies that an identifier is to represent a constant value. Thus, although the identity declaration

> **int** *k* = *15*

seems quite similar to an initializing variable declaration (:= having been replaced by =), it has a completely different effect. Unlike the other declarations we have met, it does not cause the generation of a name. The identifier *k* is called a CONSTANT rather than a variable and has the mode **int** rather than **ref int**. It is in effect a synonym for the denotation *15* and may subsequently be used as such in the program. Its value cannot be changed in any way; for example, the erroneous statements

> *k* := *0*
> *read* (*k*)

are as meaningless as

> *15* := *0*

read (15)

When a constant appears in a formula, as in

$$x := k + 5$$

dereferencing is neither necessary nor possible.

As for the expression to the right of the symbol = in an identity declaration, the rules are the same as for initializing declarations; the declared constant thereafter represents whatever value is yielded. It may subsequently be used in other declarations, as in the sequence

    int $a = -200$;
    int b; *read* (b);
    int $c := a + b$;
    int $d = a - c$

Identity declarations can be combined, as in

    int *one* = *1*, *two* = *2*, *three* = *3*

Again, none of the expressions should contain a constant which is declared in the same phrase. Variables and constants must be declared in separate phrases. Thus

    int $a := 0, b = 10, c$

is erroneous and must be replaced by, for example,

    int $a := 0, c$; **int** $b = 10$

Only integers have been considered in this section, but there should be no difficulty in applying the constructions for initializing and identity declarations to other modes.

For reasons of efficiency, constants rather than variables should be used to represent values which are used several times in a program but which never change. They are also useful as mnemonic representations for important constant values. In this connection, there are a number of predefined constants, some of which are called ENVIRONMENT ENQUIRIES because they represent certain values which depend upon the environment in which the program is run. A few of the predefined constants are summarized below:

Constant	Mode	Value
max int	**int**	the largest value of mode **int**
max real	**real**	the largest value of mode **real**
small real	**real**	the smallest real value which has a different effect from *0* when added to or subtracted from *1*
int width	**int**	the number of decimal digits in *max int*
real width	**int**	the number of significant digits in the mantissa of a real number
exp width	**int**	the number of digits in the exponent of *max real*
pi	**real**	$\pi\,(3.14\ldots)$
blank	**char**	" ⌴ "
max abs char	**int**	the largest integer yielded by **abs** *c*, where *c* yields a character (see 1.5.2)
error char	**char**	(see 2.2.2)

The environment enquiries can sometimes be used in such a way as to ensure that a program can be run without change in different environments. The following program merely prints their values:

> (*print* ((*max int, max real, small real,*
>   *int width, real width, exp width,*
>   *max abs char, error char*)))

2.3.4 Non-numeric Examples (SCO)

There are some special rules for the input of character and string values. If the mode of *c* is **ref char**, then the statement *read*(*c*) causes the next character in the input stream to be assigned to *c*. Spaces are not skipped: if the next character is a space, then " ⌴ " will be the new value of *c*. The character is not enclosed by quotes in the data, and the current position is advanced by just one character. Thus if the next character happens to be a quote, the resulting value of *c* will be " " " ". If the end of a line of data has been reached, the character that is input will be the first one in the next line.

In the case of strings, there must be some limit on the number of characters read, or the value would have to be taken as the entire unread portion of the data stream, however long it may be. In fact, the statement *read*(*s*), where *s* is a string variable, inputs characters, including any spaces and quotes, only up to the end of the current line. To input successive lines as string values, *newline* must be used, as in *read* ((*s1*, *newline*, *s2*))

The following simple program inputs three lines and prints them, each preceded by an appropriate heading:

```
( string heading = " ⌣ input ⌣ line: ⌣ ";
  string line; read (line);
  print (("first ⌣", heading, line));
  read ((newline, line));
  print ((newline, "second", heading, line));
  read ((newline, line));
  print ((newline, "third ⌣", heading, line)) )
```

Note the use of the string constant *heading* as a mnemonic for a value which is used at three different places. If the data supplied to the program is

```
this is
3 lines
of data
```

then the output will appear as follows:

```
first  input line:  this is
second input line:  3 lines
third  input line:  of data
```

In the following program, the variable *line* is declared with an initial value which is replaced by various other values in subsequent statements:

```
( char c1, c2, c3; read((c1, c2, c3));
  string line := c1 +c2 +c3;
  print (line);
  print ((newline, line timesab 2));
  print ((newline, "the ⌣" plusto line));
  line[5:7] := line[1:3];
  print ((newline, line)) )
```

It may be verified that with the input

```
tom
```

the program produces the following output:

```
tom
```

```
tomtom
the tomtom
the thetom
```

Exercises

1. Using string constants, write a program which will produce the following output:

```
****
********
************
********
****
```

2. It is required to input two eighty-character lines from cards and print the characters forty to a line. Write programs for this using (a) two string variables and (b) one string variables.
3. Using one string variable, write a concise program to print the first three lines shown in question 1.

2.3.5 Additional Numeric Facilities (NUM)

A number of procedures are available to aid in writing programs for mathematical or scientific problems. When the procedure *sqrt* is called, for example, it calculates the positive square root of the value (which must not be negative) yielded by the actual parameter supplied to it. Unlike the transput procedures, a call of *sqrt* yields a value (the square root of the actual parameter) and is thus an expression rather than a statement. It is normally used in much the same way as a variable, constant, or denotation, as the following phrases illustrate:

> x **plusab** *sqrt* (y)
> **real** $x := 2 * sqrt (x * (y + 5)) + 1$
> *print* (*sqrt* (x))
> $x := sqrt (sqrt (pi))$

In the last example, *sqrt* (*pi*) is elaborated first, yielding a value for the actual parameter of a second call of *sqrt*, so that the effect of the statement is to assign the fourth root of π to x.

The predefined procedures for mathematical functions are summarized in the following table:

Procedure identifier	Value yielded with actual parameter x
sqrt	$\sqrt{x}$
exp	e^x
ln	$\log_e x$
cos	$\cos x$
arc cos	$\cos^{-1} x$
sin	$\sin x$
arc sin	$\sin^{-1} x$
tan	$\tan x$
arc tan	$\tan^{-1} x$

In each case, the values yielded by an actual parameter and by a call as a whole have the mode **real**. An integer expression can be used as an actual parameter, for its value will be widened when the call is elaborated. Those values which represent angles are assumed to be expressed in radians rather than degrees (π radians $= 180$ degrees). A call of *arc cos* always yields a value between 0 and π inclusive, while *arc sin* and *arc tan* yield values between $-\pi/2$ and $\pi/2$ inclusive.

The following program inputs an angle expressed in degrees and prints the values of the corresponding trigonometric functions:

```
( real angle; read (angle);
  angle timesab pi / 180;
  real sine = sin (angle), cosine = cos (angle),
      tangent = tan (angle);
  real cosec = 1 / sine, secant = 1 / cosine,
      cotan = 1 / tangent;
  print ((sine, cosine, tangent, cosec, secant, cotan)) )
```

Note the use of constants: there is no need to declare *sine*, *cosine*, and *tangent* as variables since each of them has only one value during elaboration; this might not be the case in a more complicated program. The third phrase, which converts the angle from degrees to radians, makes use of the predefined constant *pi*. The constants *cosec*, *secant*, and *cotan* serve only to make the program more readable; they could be eliminated by inserting the expressions for their values directly into the output statement.

As a second example, here is a program which inputs the coefficients a, b, and c of a quadratic equation

$$ax^2 + bx + c = 0$$

and prints the values of the two roots:

```
( real a, b, c; read ((a, b, c));
  real disc  =  sqrt (b * b  -  4 * a * c), a2  =  2 * a;
  print ((( (-b  +  disc) / a2,
            (-b  -  disc) / a2)) )
```

This program will not work if the equation has complex roots, since the actual parameter of *sqrt* will then be negative. Constants (*disc* and *a2*) have again been used to represent computed values. In the following program, which solves two quadratic equations, variables are used for this purpose:

```
( real a, b, c; read ((a, b, c));
  real disc := sqrt(b * b  -  4 * a * c), a2 := 2 * a;
  print (((-b  +  disc) / a2, (-b  -  disc) / a2));
  read ((a, b, c));
  disc := sqrt(b * b  -  4 * a * c); a2 := 2 * a;
  print (((-b  +  disc) / a2, (-b  -  disc) / a2)) )
```

Exercises

1. Write a program which inputs the lengths a, b, and c of the sides of a triangle and outputs the area, which is equal to

$$\sqrt{s(s - a)(s - b)(s - c)} \qquad \text{where} \qquad s = \tfrac{1}{2}(a + b + c)$$

2. Write a program which finds the area of two triangles as above.
3. Write a program which inputs two sets of values for x and y and outputs the corresponding values of the expression

$$\frac{1}{2\pi} [e^{x-y} \sin(x+y) \cos(x+y) \log_e \cos^{-1}x]$$

Chapter 3
Loops and Multiple Values

3.1 Clause Structure and Ranges

Only rarely can practical computational tasks be carried out by the simple straight-line type of program. In more complicated programs, the sequential elaboration of phrases is modified by the use of language features which specify other rules for the flow of control from one phrase to another. One of the most important of these control devices is the LOOP, a sequence of phrases which appear only once in the program but may be elaborated many times. In this chapter we shall see how to compose some loops and use them effectively in programs. First it is necessary to introduce some more technical terms related to the overall structure of programs.

A SERIES (sometimes called a SERIAL CLAUSE) is a sequence of one or more phrases separated by semicolons. The last phrase in a series must be a unit, and the mode and value of the series are defined to be the mode and value of this final unit. A CLOSED CLAUSE is a type of unit obtained by enclosing a series either by parentheses or by **begin** and **end**. Thus the straight-line programs of the previous chapter all consist of closed clauses. A closed clause constitutes the RANGE of all the variables and constants declared in it by the means described in 1.4 and 2.3.3. These identifiers are said to be LOCAL to the range in which they are declared; a name is also said to be local to the range in which it is generated.

All this is largely irrelevant in the case of straight-line programs with a single range. However, a range may have other ranges contained in it, so that the following is the structural outline of a valid program:

```
begin
   int x;
   ... ;
   begin
      int y;
      ...
   end;
```

```
    . . .
  end
```

Observe the punctuation carefully; the inner closed clause acts as a single statement of the outer series. Its **end** symbol is not preceded by a semicolon since there is nothing to go on to in the inner series; however, it is followed by a semicolon because in this case there are further phrases in the outer series. The variable y is local to the inner range; i.e., the name it represents is generated at the beginning and ceases to exist at the end of the range's elaboration. Thus it cannot appear in any phrase outside this closed clause. The variable x, on the other hand, is GLOBAL to the inner range and may appear anywhere in the program.

Now consider the following program outline:

```
  begin
    int x;
    ...;
    begin
      int x;
      ...
    end;
    ...
  end
```

There is a name represented by x which is local to the inner range. This name is completely distinct from the one generated in the outer range, even though they share the same identifier. The only difference from the previous example is that now the name generated in the outer range is inaccessible during elaboration of the inner closed clause. This is so because all occurrences of the identifier x therein are assumed to correspond to the local name. Upon leaving the inner range, the local name ceases to exist and the global name may again be accessed by subsequent phrases. It should be fairly clear how these 'scope rules' for names may be generalized to cover more complicated cases of nested ranges.

No identifier may be declared more than once at the same scope level, i.e., in the same series. Moreover, if a non-predefined identifier is used but not declared in a given range, then it must be declared in some enclosing range. A predefined identifier such as *read* may be redeclared in some range, but its predefined meaning will then be lost within that range.

We have mentioned the use of closed clauses as statements. They can also be used as expressions, where the value yielded is defined as the value of the enclosed series, i.e., the value of the final unit:

```
begin
  int x;
  x := begin
           int y, z;
           read ((y, z));
           y + z
       end;
  print ((x, 2 * x))
end
```

In this program, x is assigned the sum of two input values. The variables y and z are local to the closed clause which acts as an expression within the assignation.

It is possible for a closed clause to contain nothing but a final unit:

```
begin
  int x, y, z;
  read ((y, z));
  x := 2 * begin
              y + z
           end;
  print ((x, 2 * x))
end
```

This can be written more compactly as

```
( int x, y, z;
  read ((y, z));
  x := 2 * (y + z);
  print ((x, 2 * x)) )
```

Thus we see that the parenthesized formulas first introduced in 1.5 are really simple examples of closed clauses containing no declarations. Their purpose is not to set up inner ranges but to alter the effect of the priorities of operators.

Exercises

1. Point out the errors in the following programs:
   (a) (int $x := 5$;
     (int y;
     $y := x$)
     $x := y$)

(b) (**int** $x := 5$;
    begin
      int x;
      $x := 5$;
    end;
    print (x))
(c) (**int** x;
    $x :=$ (**int** y; *read* (y));
    print (x))
(d) ((**int** x; *read*(x));
    (**int** $y := 5$; *print* $(x + y)$))

2. Rewrite the last example in this section using a constant for x.

3.2 Unconditional Loops

3.2.1 Simple Loop Clauses

A loop of a very simple type can be expressed in Algol 68 by a LOOP CLAUSE of the form

    to integer-expression **do** series **od**

All loop clauses contain the indicants **do** and **od**. Those of this particular form are elaborated as follows: the expression following the **to** is first elaborated to yield some integer value, and the series following the **do** is then elaborated this number of times in succession. In the case of

    to 5 **do** *print* (x) **od**

the value yielded by x will be printed 5 times. The series delimited by **do** and **od** constitutes the range of any identifiers declared in it. A loop clause as a whole is a statement, i.e., a unit of mode **void**.

In the following loop, ten numbers are input and added to the value referred to by the variable x:

    to 10 **do** *read* (y); x **plusab** y **od**

The number of repetitions is not necessarily known at the time the program is written, as in the following example:

    $x := 0$; *read* (n);
    to n **do** *read* (y); x **plusab** y **od**

Here it is assumed that the first number in the input data gives the number of subsequent numbers to be added. But when elaboration of the loop clause begins, the number of repetitions is known and fixed. It cannot then be changed, even by including within the series an assignation which changes the value of n (although n would then refer to a different value).

It is often useful to be able to access the number of the current repetition. This is possible in loop clauses of the form

> **for** integer-identifier **to** integer-expression
> **do** series **od**

The following example contains such a construct:

> **int** $s := 0$, $ss := 0$;
> **for** i **to** 10 **do**
> $\quad$ s **plusab** i;
> $\quad$ ss **plusab** $i * i$
> **od**

The identifier i is a constant rather than a variable; hence its value cannot be changed in any way inside the series. It is not explicitly declared anywhere, but is implicitly declared by a suitable identity declaration which we may consider to be elaborated just before each repetition. That is,

> **int** $i = 1$

is implicitly elaborated just before the first repetition; then

> **int** $i = 2$

is implicitly elaborated just before the second repetition, and so on. The scope of i is restricted to the loop itself, so that there is no conflict with any other i explicitly declared in an outer range (the latter would of course be inaccessible inside the loop). The effect of the example is to assign the sum of the integers between 1 and 10 to s and the sum of their squares to ss.

The construction
> **for** i **to** 10

is in fact an abbreviation for any of the following three constructions:

> **for** i **from** 1 **to** 10
> **for** i **by** 1 **to** 10
> **for** i **from** 1 **by** 1 **to** 10

We are now considering loop clauses of the general form

> **for** integer-identifier
> **from** integer-expression
> **by** integer-expression
> **to** integer-expression
> **do** series
> **od**

or, for short,

> **for I from J by K to L do S od**

The values yielded by J, K, and L determine the number of repetitions of S and the value represented by I during each repetition. The expressions J, K, and L are first elaborated. Assuming that the value of K is positive, S is then repeatedly elaborated with I representing the successive values in the following sequence which are less than or equal to the value of L:

$$J, J + K, J + 2K, J + 3K, \ldots$$

If K is negative, the values represented by I are those of the above which are greater than or equal to L. Note that it is possible for S not to be elaborated at all, as in

> **for** i **from** 10 **by** 1 **to** 9 **do** ... **od**

If **from** J is omitted, then **from** 1 is assumed; if **by** K is omitted, then **by** 1 is assumed. As is the case for L, changing the values inside the loop of any variables which occur in J and K will not alter the number of repetitions.

The following statements assign to ss the sum of the squares of all the even numbers between -8 and n:

> $ss := 0$;
> **for** z **from** -8 **by** 2 **to** n
> **do** ss **plusab** $z * z$ **od**

In the next example, the squares of the odd positive numbers less than 100 are printed in descending order:

> **for** q **from** 99 **by** -2 **to** 0 **do** $print$ $(q * q)$ **od**

Exercises

1. Point out the errors in each of the following loop clauses:

   (a) **to** *100* **do**; *read* (*x*); *print* (*x*) **od**
   (b) **for** *i* **to** *n* **do**
       read (*i*);
       x **plusab** *i*;
       i := *0* **od**
   (c) **for** *j* **by** 5 **from** *n* — *m* **to** *n* **do** *print* (*j* ∗ *j*) **od**

2. Assuming in each case that the initial value of *x* is *0*, what is its value after the elaboration of each of the following?

   (a) **to** *10* **do** *x* **plusab** *1* **od**
   (b) **to** *x* **do** *x* **plusab** *1* **od**
   (c) **from** −*4* **by** *2* **to** *2* **do** *x* **plusab** *1* **od**
   (d) **from** *x* **to** *x* + *10* **do** *x* **plusab** *1* **od**

3.2.2 The Necessity for and Use of Loops∗

It is frequently necessary to have the same, or nearly the same, computation performed many times in succession. This arises partly from the fact that most of the tasks which are carried out by computers have highly repetitious aspects (and hence are tedious from a human point of view). As a very simple example, suppose that we wish to input a long sequence of numbers and print out the result of doubling each of them. If there are only five numbers, the following statements would be necessary in a straight-line program:

```
read (x);
print (2 ∗ x);
read (x);
print (2 ∗ x);
read (x);
print (2 ∗ x);
read (x);
print (2 ∗ x);
read (x);
print (2 ∗ x)
```

If there are 1000 numbers, the task of coding a straight-line program becomes unmanageable, and if the number is not known at the time the program is written, it becomes logically impossible. These problems are easily overcome by the use of the loop clauses

to *1000* **do** *read* (x); *print* $(2 * x)$ **od**

and

to *n* **do** *read* (x); *print* $(2 * x)$ **od**

In general, whenever it is necessary to have identical groups of phrases repeated some specifiable number of times, a loop clause of the form

to L **do** S **od**

can be used.

It is very common for loops to contain statements which change the values of variables in a cumulative fashion, as in forming the sum of a set of numbers. The following statements find the average of *n* numbers:

$s := 0$;
to *n* **do** *read*(x); *s* **plusab** *x* **od**;
$avg := s / n$

The initializing statement

$s := 0$

is necessary for the statement

s **plusab** *x*

to be meaningful the first time it is elaborated. This example also illustrates how a loop clause as a whole functions like any other statement in the program: in this case it is followed by a semicolon because another statement follows it.

The more complicated forms of loop clause introduced in the previous section are used in cases where similar but not identical groups of phrases are to be repeated. For example, the following sequence sums successive integers:

$s := 0$;
s **plusab** *1*;
s **plusab** *2*;

s **plusab** *3*;

. . .

The regular pattern of the operands *1, 2, 3, . . .*, which correspond to repetition number, is captured by means of a **for** part in the loop clause:

s := 0;
for *i* **to** *n* **do** *s* **plusab** *i* **od**

The **from** and **by** parts may be used when the relationship between repetition number and operand pattern is not so direct. In practice, however, the pattern

from *1* **by** *1*

is by far the most common and so is often omitted.

Like any other statement, a loop clause may be contained in the series of a loop clause, giving rise to nested loops. Loops can be nested to any depth, permitting a great deal of work to be done by a short piece of program: an inner loop is completely re-elaborated, with all its repetitions, for each repetition of the enclosing loop. The following program prints *50* copies of a table of squares of integers between *1* and *50*:

```
( to 50 do
    print (newpage);
    for n to 50 do
        print ((n, n * n, newline))
    od
od )
```

When writing loops, some care should be taken with regard to efficiency. For example, in the loop

to *100* **do** $x := x \uparrow (y * y - z * z)$ **od**

the expression

$y * y - z * z$

is elaborated *100* times even though it must yield the same value each time. The loop should be replaced by something like

$yyzz := y * y - z * z$;

```
to 100 do x := x ↑ yyzz od
```

In general, invariant subexpressions should be computed outside loops
with the aid of auxiliary variables or constants.

The types of loop introduced in this chapter have greatly increased the
potential power of our programs. They are limited by the fact that the
number of repetitions of a loop is determined once and for all at the beginning of its elaboration. Loops without this limitation will be considered in
Chapter 4.

Exercises

1. Write statements to compute the factorial f of a positive integer referred
to by n.
2. Write a program which reads *100* numbers and prints their factorials.

3.2.3 Examples: String Manipulation (SCO)

We are not yet in a position to undertake any very realistic examples of
complete programs in this area, but we may consider some computations
which could form parts of such programs.

Suppose we have a string with at least three characters and wish to print
all of its substrings of length *3* on separate lines. If *str* refers to the string,
then the first substring is yielded by *str*[1:3], the second by *str*[2:4], and
so on. If the string is read as data and is of unknown length, the last substring
is given by

> *str* [**upb** *str* − 2 : **upb** *str*]

A loop will be needed to extract all the substrings and it will have to contain a
for part. The following program carries out the required task:

```
( string str; read (str);
  for i to upb str − 2 do
    print ((str [i : i + 2], newline))
  od )
```

If the process is to be carried out for many strings, each of which is taken
from a line of input, the program contains nested loops:

```
( string str;
  int n; read ((n, newline));
  to n do
    read ((str, newline));
```

```
    for i to upb str  − 2 do
        print ((str [i : i + 2], newline))
    od
od )
```

As a second example, consider the problem of reversing the order of the characters in a string. This might be useful, for instance, in a program which analyzes word suffixes, where the end of a string is the important part. One method is to build a new string character by character, as in the following program:

```
( string str, rstr := " "; read (str);
    for i from upb str by − 1 to 1 do
        rstr plusab str[i] od;
    print (rstr) )
```

Exercises

1. If a tail of a string is defined as any substring which includes the last character of the string, write a program which reads a string and prints each of its tails on a separate line.
2. Write a program which reads a string, inserts a blank after each character, and prints the result fifty times.

3.2.4 Examples: Statistical Calculations (NUM)

Suppose that we have some data in the order

$$n, x_1, x_2, \ldots, x_n$$

where n is an integer and $x_1, x_2, \ldots, x_n$ are real numbers. Then the following program computes the mean (or average) m of the real numbers:

```
( real x, s := 0;
    int n; read (n);
    to n do read (x); s plusab x od;
    print (s / n) )
```

The variance of a set of numbers is defined as the mean of their squares minus the square of their mean. In order to compute the variance as well as the mean, then, the sum of the squares must be formed as well as the sum of the numbers themselves. This cannot be done simply by adding some statements at the end of the above program because all the values of x except the last are no longer available. This problem could be overcome using multiple values, which are introduced in the next section. In this case, however, we may accumulate both sums simultaneously using only one loop:

```
( real x, s := 0, ss := 0;
  int n; read (n);
  to n do
     read (x);
     s plusab x          ¢ sum ¢;
     ss plusab x * x     ¢ sum of squares ¢
  od;
  real m = s / n;
  print (("mean ⌐ = ⌐", m, newline,
          "var ⌐ = ⌐", ss / n − m * m)) )
```

Exercises

1. Given data in the order

$$n, x_1, y_1, x_2, y_2, \ldots, x_n, y_n,$$

write a program to determine the line of least squares fit. (If p is the sum of the x's, q the sum of the y's, r the sum of the squares of the x's and s the sum of the products of the corresponding x's and y's, then the coefficients a and b of the line are given by the equations

$$q = na + pb$$
$$s = pa + rb$$

The program should print the values of a and b.)

3.3 Multiple Values

3.3.1 Introduction

A MULTIPLE VALUE, or MULTIPLE for short, is a set of values which all have the same mode and which are arranged or numbered in a certain way. Each value is said to be an ELEMENT of the multiple. The elaboration of the variable declaration

$$[1:100] \textbf{ int } a$$

involves the allocation of storage for *100* integer elements which will collectively be referred to by *a*. The mode of the multiple is []**int**, pronounced 'row of integer', and the mode of its name *a* is **ref**[]**int**; these modes are independent of the number of elements in the multiple.

The multiple referred to by *a* may be thought of as a row of integers occupying positions numbered from *1* to *100*. Each element has its own name, which may be written as an expression (e.g., the multiple variable *a*) yielding the name of the whole multiple followed by the element's position number in square brackets or parentheses. Such a construct is called a SLICE and is a type of unit. Thus the names of the elements of *a* are yielded by the slices

$$a[1] \quad a[2] \quad a[3] \quad \ldots \quad a[100]$$

The mode of each slice is **ref int**. The position numbers in brackets are called SUBSCRIPTS. The valid subscript values in this case range between *1* and *100*; i.e., the LOWER BOUND of the multiple is *1* and the UPPER BOUND is *100*. Any integer expression may be used as a subscript; it will be elaborated and combined with the name of the multiple to yield the name of an element.

When a lower bound is *1*, it may be omitted from the declaration together with the colon, so that

[*100*] **int** *a*

is equivalent to the previous declaration. Here are some more examples of declarations of multiple variables:

[− *10:10*] **int** *b*
[*0* : *i* ∗ *j*] **int** *c*, *d*
[*50*] **real** *e*

The value of *b* will consist of 21 integer elements whose names are yielded by the slices

$$b[-10] \quad b[-9] \quad \ldots \quad b[0] \quad \ldots \quad b[9] \quad b[10]$$

For *c* and *d*, the lower bound is *0*, and the upper bound is the integer yielded by *i* ∗ *j*. Any integer expression can be used to specify a bound in a declarer for a multiple variable, subject to the usual requirement that all variables and constants contained in it must have been declared and must have suitable values at the time of the declaration's elaboration. The mode of *e* as declared above if **ref**[ ]**real**; the *50* elements in its value all have the mode **real**, and the slices

$$e[1] \quad e[2] \quad e[3] \quad \ldots \quad e[50]$$

all have the mode **ref real**.

Each slice yielding the name of an element of a multiple can be used in exactly the same contexts within a program as a simple variable of the same mode. The following examples illustrate how names of elements can acquire and yield values in the elaboration of formulas, assignations, transput statements, variable declarations, and identity declarations:

$a[1] * (a[50] - 5)$
$a[1 + a[i + j]]$
$i := a[1] + a[2] + a[3]$
$a[i]$ **plusab** 1
read $(a[1])$
read $((b[-1], b[0], b[1]))$
print $((c[1] + b[2] + 1, a[20]))$
int $i := a[j] + b[j]$
int $j = a[2]\uparrow 3$
$[a[5]]$ **int** $z1, z2, z3$

All the multiples considered above are ONE-DIMENSIONAL; i.e., any of their elements can be accessed using only one subscript. The following declaration defines a variable for a TWO-DIMENSIONAL multiple:

$[0:99, 100]$ **int** aa

The declarer specifies two pairs of lower and upper bounds (the second lower bound is 1), and each element can be accessed with the aid of two subscripts. Space will be allocated for 10,000 elements collectively referred to by aa. The mode of the multiple is written as [,] **int** ('row row of integer'), and the mode of its name is **ref[,]int**. The multiple may be thought of as a rectangular array of integers where the positions along a row are numbered from 1 to 100 and the positions down a column from 0 to 99. In a slice yielding the name of an element, the two subscripts are separated by a comma; the second subscript gives the position number from left to right, and the first subscript gives the position number from top to bottom. Thus the names of the elements of aa may be written as follows:

$aa[0,1]$	$aa[0,2]$	$aa[0,3]$	$\ldots$	$aa[0,100]$
$aa[1,1]$	$aa[1,2]$	$aa[1,3]$	$\ldots$	$aa[1,100]$
$\vdots$	$\vdots$	$\vdots$		$\vdots$
$aa[99,1]$	$aa[99,2]$	$aa[99,3]$	$\ldots$	$aa[99,100]$

Each slice is again of mode **ref int** and may appear in any context where a simple integer variable could be used.

Although one- and two-dimensional multiples are adequate for most applications, it is possible to have any number of dimensions:

[0.4, 0:5, 0:6] **int** *aaa*
[m1:n1, m2:n2, m3:n3, m4:n4, m5:n5] **real** *x*

The respective modes of *aaa* and *x* are **ref**[,,]**int** ('reference to row row row of integer') and **ref**[,,,,]**real**. The properties of many-dimensional multiples are a straightforward generalization of the properties of one- and two-dimensional multiples.

3.3.2 Multiples and their Use with Loops*

The main advantage of multiples is that they enable us to group together a large set of values under one name in such a way that any value can be accessed by its position in the set. This is also commonly done in mathematical notation, where a large number of variables of similar characteristics are written with subscripts, as in

$$x_1, x_2, x_3, \ldots, x_n,$$

instead of using n distinct simple variables. If the value of n is not known, then the use of simple variables alone is not merely inconvenient but logically impossible. Similarly, in Algol 68, the declaration

[100] **int** *a*

saves us from having to declare *100* distinct variables for integer values, and the sequence

int *n*; *read* (*n*); [*n*] **int** *b*

has no equivalent without multiple variables.

Two-dimensional multiples correspond to the use of doubly-subscripted variables in mathematical notation:

$$y_{11}, y_{12}, \ldots, y_{1n}, y_{21}, y_{22}, \ldots, y_{2n}, \ldots,$$
$$y_{n1}, y_{n2}, \ldots, y_{nn}$$

The programming of matrix computations (3.3.8) is an important application here.

In a slice yielding the name of an element, it is important to distinguish the value of a subscript from the value of the element. The subscript simply serves to pick out one of the values in the multiple. Thus, if the value of i is 5, then the value of $a[i]$ is not necessarily 5; it is whatever value $a[5]$ has most recently acquired.

Care should be taken to ensure that a subscript value will never be outside the bounds specified in the declaration for the relevant multiple. For example, the following program would lead to trouble when executed:

```
( [3] int a;
  read ((a[3], a[2], a[1]));
  for i to 4 do print (a[i]) od )
```

Mistakes of this sort are frequently made in larger programs.

The above program illustrates another point about multiples: they are very often used in conjunction with loops of the forms described earlier in this chapter. This arises from the fact that a multiple usually serves to store a set of values which are all to be manipulated in the same way. Thus it is natural to use loop clauses for these repetitive calculations, where the identifiers in the **for** parts are used as subscripts. For example, here is a program which inputs values for two multiple variables x and y in the order

$$x_1, y_1, x_2, y_2, \ldots, x_{50}, y_{50}$$

and prints each multiple in a separate column in reverse order:

```
( [50] int x, y;
  for i to 50 do
    read ((x[i], y[i])) od;
  for i from 50 by −1 to 1 do
    print ((x[i], y[i], newline)) od )
```

With two-dimensional multiples, nested loops are often used in order to vary both subscripts throughout their ranges of allowed values and thus process all elements of the multiple. The following statements form the sum of all the elements in a multiple referred to by a with ten rows and five columns:

```
sum := 0;
for i to 10 do
  for j to 5 do
    sum plusab a[i,j]
  od
od
```

The next example is a statement which calculates and prints the sum of the elements in each row:

```
for i to 10 do
    sum := 0;
    for j to 5 do sum plusab a[i,j] od;
    print (sum)
od
```

Note that the ·initialization and output statements are inside the outer loop but outside the inner loop. The efficiency of the last two examples can be improved by the use of a technique described in 3.3.5.

It should be appreciated that multiples can take up a great deal of memory. For example, a variable declared as

[100, 100] **int** bb

will require at least as much space as 10,000 individual integers. If there are several such multiples, it may be expensive or impossible to run the program on a given computer system. The number of large multiples should therefore be kept to a minimum, perhaps by using the same multiple variable for different purposes in different parts of a program. Alternatively, space can sometimes be saved by declaring large multiple variables in disjoint ranges, as in the following program outline:

```
begin
    begin
        [100, 100] int aa;
        . . .
    end;
    begin
        [30, 40, 50] int xyz;
        . . .
    end
end
```

Exercises

1. Write a program which inputs 20 integer values and prints the difference (mode **real**) between each value and the average of the values.
2. Write a program which inputs integer data in the order

$$n, a_0, b_0, a_1, b_1, a_2, b_2, \ldots, a_n, b_n$$

and prints the values of $a_i + b_i$ and $a_i - b_i$ in two columns for decreasing values of i.

3. Using loop clauses and a two-dimensional multiple as a table of values
    for a^b where a and b are integers between 1 and 5, write a program which
    prints the sums of the values in each row on one line and the sums of the
    values in each column on a second line.

3.3.3. Manipulation of Complete Muliples

We have seen that elements of multiple values can be used in the same
way as simple values. In this and the following three sections, we consider
more powerful methods of manipulating multiples. We shall continue to
work mainly with integer multiples, since the rules for other row modes are
analogous. It is in fact possible to specify a multiple of values of any mode in
the language, including another row mode. Thus

   [*m*] [*n*] **int** *ab*

generates the name of a one-dimensional multiple of mode [] []**int** ('row of
integer') with *m* elements, each of which is a one-dimensional multiple
of mode []**int** with *n* integer elements. The slice *ab*[*1*], of mode **ref**[]**int**,
yields the name of the first of these integer multiples. This slice can thus
itself be subscripted, so that *ab*[*1*] [*1*] (which is equivalent to (*ab*[*1*]) [*1*]),
of mode **ref int**, yields the name of the first element in the first multiple.

The use of multiple variables without subscripts often results in less
programming effort. For example, if *a* has been declared as

   [*m*:*n*] **int** *a*

then the statement *read*(*a*) is equivalent to

   for *i* **from** *m* **to** *n* **do** *read* (*a*[*i*]) **od**

Similarly, if *p* and *q* are simple variables, the statement

   read ((*p*, *a*, *q*))

will input a value for *p*, followed by $n - m + 1$ values for *a*, followed
by a value for *q*. For a two-dimensional multiple declared as

   [*m*:*n*, *p*:*q*] **int** *aa*

the statement *read* (*aa*) is equivalent to

   for *i* **from** *m* **to** *n* **do**

```
    for j from p to q do
       read (aa[i,j])
    od
od
```

Whenever a many-dimensional multiple variable appears in an input statement, the implied ordering of the element names is that in which the leftmost subscript varies the least rapidly and the rightmost subscript the most rapidly.

These rules apply equally well to output statements. The statement

   $print\ ((a, newline, aa))$

has the same effect as

```
for i from m to n do print (a[i]) od;
print (newline);
for i from m to n do
   for j from p to q do
      print (aa[i,j])
   od
od
```

The automatic decomposition of multiples or names of multiples for purposes of transput is called STRAIGHTENING.

Compatible multiple variables can be used in some simple assignments. Suppose the following declarations are in effect:

   $[m:n]$ **int** a, b;
   $[m:n]$ **real** c;
   $[p:q]$ **int** d;
   $[m:n, p:q]$ **int** e, f

Then the statement $a := b$ has the same effect as

   for i **from** m **to** n **do** $a[i] := b[i]$ **od**

and $e := f$ has the same effect as

```
for i from m to n do
   for j from p to q do e[i,j] := f[i,j] od
od
```

The dimensionality and bounds of the multiples given by the two sides of the assignation must match exactly; thus $a := d$ is illegal (unless the values of m and p and of n and q are equal). Both $c := a$ and $a := c$ are illegal, and so is

$a :=$ **entier** c

because **entier**, like all the other arithmetic operators we have met, is not defined for operands of mode [ ]**real** or any other row mode; we must use a loop clause in this case.

Instead of using a multiple variable on the right side, it is possible to specify each value separately using a ROW DISPLAY, which is an expression consisting of a set of two or more expressions separated by commas and enclosed by parentheses (or **begin** and **end**). If we have the declarations

int $p := 15$;
[3] **int** a;
[5] **real** b

then the following are valid assignations containing row displays:

$a := (4, 5, 6)$;
$b := (a[i], 6.4, p + 3, 0, 0)$

A row display yields a multiple with lower bound 1 and an upper bound equal to the number of expressions it contains. The name yielded by the left side must refer to a multiple with the same bounds. In the case of two-dimensional multiples, we may write row displays containing expressions which themselves yield multiples, as in

$bb := ((45,36), (97,12), (52,0))$

which could be used to assign values to a multiple name created by

[3,2] **int** bb

A row display may be used only in contexts where all coercions are permitted; in particular, it cannot be subscripted or used as an operand. A means of overcoming this restriction is described in 6.2.1.

Initializing declarations of multiple variables are analogous to the above assignations. The following sequence contains some examples:

[4] **int** $a := (21, 22, 23, 24)$;
[2,4] **int** $aa := (a, (6, 7, 8, 9))$;
[4] **real** $c := (a[1], a[2], a[3], a[4])$

If we wish to initialize all but one or two elements or rows of a multiple, we can make use of the symbol **skip** or $\searrow$, a special unit which yields an undefined value of any required mode:

[4] **int** $d := (100, 450,$ **skip**$, 600)$;
[3, 4] **int** $dd :=. ((50, 60, 70, 80), a,$ **skip**$)$

The **skip** facility is useful in many contexts. When it is used as a dummy statement, nothing is done during its elaboration.

The identity declaration

[ ]**int** $p2 = (2, 4, 8, 16, 32)$

is analogous to other identity declarations. The identifier $p2$ represents a multiple constant of mode [ ] **int** and bounds [1:5], which are taken from the right side. Note that no bounds are included in the declarer (although a colon is optional). The slices

$p2[1]$ $p2[2]$ $p2[3]$ $p2[4]$ $p2[5]$

are all constants of mode **int** yielding different powers of 2. We can equally well write

[ ] **int** $a = b$

where b must yield a multiple of mode [ ]**int**. The bounds of a will be the same as those of b. The identity declaration

[,] **int** $ee = dd$

specifies a two-dimensional constant multiple; the comma in the declarer must be present.

Exercises

1. Write a program which inputs integer data in the order

$$a_1, a_2, \ldots, a_{10}, b_1, b_2, \ldots, b_{10}$$

and prints on four successive lines the values of $a_i, b_i, a_i + b_i$, and $a_i - b_i$, where $1 \leq i \leq 10$.
2. Using one row display, write a program which prints a multiple consisting of the first ten prime numbers on each of fifty lines, in alternately ascending and descending order.

3.3.4 Manipulation of Parts of Multiples

A TRIMMER is a pair of integer expressions, separated by a colon, which may be used in a slice to specify a subset of a multiple value. If *a* is declared as

[2:20] **int** *a*

then the slice *a*[5:10] yields the name of the multiple consisting of the elements of *a* with position numbers 5 through 10. Unlike a slice such as *a*[5], the mode of this slice is **ref**[ ]**int** as is *a* itself. An expression in a trimmer may be omitted if it is equal to the corresponding bound in the complete multiple; thus *a*[5] is equivalent to *a*[2:5] and *a*[15:] is equivalent to *a*[15:20]. The lower bounds of the submultiples referred to by all these slices are *1* and the upper bounds are adjusted accordingly. The bounds of the multiple referred to by *a*[5:10], for example, are [1:6]; consequently,

[6] **int** *b* := *a*[5:10]

is a valid phrase.

If both expressions are absent from a trimmer, and if the colon is then also omitted, there is no adjustment of the bounds. Thus the bounds of *a*[ ], like *a* itself, are [2:20], while those of *a*[2:20] or *a*[:] are [1:19]. However, adjustment can always be forced or modified to produce any desired value for the new lower bound, given by some integer expression L, by appending **at** L or @ L to the trimmer. In each of the following pairs, the slice on the left refers to a multiple with the bounds given on the right:

a[5:10 **at** 5]	[5:10]
a[:5 **at** 40]	[40:44]
a[15: **at** − 10]	[− 10:− 5]
a[**at** 1]	[1:19]

Consequently, the following sequence is valid:

[5:10] **int** *c* := *a*[5:10 **at** 5];
[ ] **real** *d* = *a*[:5 **at** 40];
[− 10:− 5] **int** *e*;
[19] **int** *f*;
e := *a*[15: **at** − 10];
f := *a*[**at** 1]

With two-dimensional multiples, pairs of trimmers may be used. Thus if *aa* is declared as

[0:9, 2:10] **int** aa

then aa[:5, 7:9 **at** 3] refers to a multiple (mode [,] **int**) with bounds [1:6, 3:5] where the elements are found in row numbers 0 through 5 and column numbers 7 through 9 of aa. Similarly, aa[8:9] has bounds [1:2,2:10] and refers to the elements in the last two rows of aa. (Note that the bounds for the second dimension have not been adjusted.)

Since a trimmed multiple is itself a multiple, it can be trimmed or subscripted. Thus we have the following pairs of equivalent slices:

a[5:10] [2]	a[6]
a[5:10 **at** 5] [6:7]	a[6:7]
aa[**at** 1, **at** 1] [1:2,]	aa[0:1, **at** 1]

If a two-dimensional multiple variable is used with one subscript and one trimmer, a one-dimensional multiple is obtained. For example, aa[9,] refers to the last row of aa, aa[,2] refers to its first column, and the declaration

[10] **int** g := aa[**at** 1, 2]

is valid. It should be clear how these concepts may be generalized to multiples of more than two dimensions.

In order to change simultaneously the values contained in part of a multiple, a slice yielding the submultiple can be used as the left side of an assignation. The adjusted bounds must match the bounds of the multiple yielded by the right side, which is assigned to the submultiple on the left as specified before the bounds adjustment. Suppose, for example, that the following declarations are in effect:

[3] **int** a;   [2:4] **int** b;
[2] **int** c;   [2:3] **int** d;
[2,3] **int** aa

Then in the assignation

a[2:3] := c

the adjusted bounds on the left, [1:2], match the bounds on the right, and a[2] and a[3] are assigned the values of c[1] and c[2] respectively. The following statements are also valid:

a[2:3 **at** 2] := d
a[2:3] := d [**at** 1]

$$a[2:3] := (10, 20)$$

We cannot have $b := a$, since the bounds do not match, but $b[\textbf{at } 1] := a$ is valid. Finally,

$$aa[2,] := a$$

changes the second row of *aa*.

Slices referring to parts of the same multiple may appear on both sides of an assignation, as in

$$a[1:2] := a[2:3]$$

This is equivalent to

$$a[1] := a[2]; a[2] := a[3]$$

and not

$$a[2] := a[3]; a[1] := a[2]$$

where the original value of $a[2]$ would be lost. On the other hand,

$$a[2:3] := a[1:2]$$

is equivalent to

$$a[3] := a[2]; a[2] := a[1]$$

since a value would be lost if copying began at the lower end.

Exercises

1. Write a program which inputs a ten-by-ten table of integer values row by row and outputs it column by column.
2. Write a program to input fifty numbers and output each consecutive group of ten on a separate line together with their sum.

3.3.5 Identity Declarations of Variables

An identity declaration in which the declarer begins with the symbol **ref** specifies that the identifier on the left side is to represent the name yielded by the right side. Thus if *i* is a variable of mode **ref int**, the declaration

ref int $j \ = \ i$

specifies that j is to represent the same name as i. The two variables will then be interchangeable in all contexts within the scope of j; they will always yield the same value and $read(j)$, for example, will have exactly the same effect as $read(i)$. Note that

ref int $j \ = \ i \ + \ k$

is invalid because the right side does not yield a name. The right side of the identity declaration

ref int $j \ = \ i := 5$

is an assignation; i and j will both represent the same name, which initially refers to 5.

These constructs are particularly useful when the right side is a slice, as in

ref int $ai \ = \ a[i]$

Now ai can be written in place of $a[i]$; this is advantageous if the latter would otherwise be elaborated several times with the same value of i, because now the subscripting is only performed once in the declaration. As a simple example,

to *10* **do** *read* $(a[5])$; *print* $(a[5])$ **od**

can be replaced by

ref int $a5 \ = \ a[5]$;
to *10* **do** *read* $(a5)$; *print* $(a5)$**od**

The identity declaration

ref[ ]int $b \ = \ a$

permits the multiple variable b to be used interchangeably with a in all contexts. Note that, as in identity declarations of multiple constants, the declarer contains no bounds. A variable for a submultiple can also be declared:

ref[ ]int $c \ = \ a[2{:}3]$

Now the bounds of c are $[1,2]$; $c[1]$ is interchangeable with $a[2]$, and $c[2]$ is interchangeable with $a[3]$.

If aa is a two-dimensional multiple variable, then

ref[ ]**int** d = $aa[2,]$

makes d refer to the second row of the multiple, so that the slices $d[i]$ and $a[2,i]$ are equivalent. Similarly,

ref[ ]**int** e = $aa[,3]$

makes e refer to the third column of the multiple, so that $e[i]$ and $aa[i,3]$ are equivalent. In each case, the first alternative is more efficient because of the reduced number of subscripts.

As an illustration of this technique, the following program is an improved version of the solution to Exercise 3 in 3.2.2:

```
begin
    [5,5] int power; int sum;
    for a to 5 do
        ref[ ]int arow = power[a,];
        for b to 5 do arow[b] := a ↑ b od
    od;
    for a to 5 do
        ref[ ]int arow = power[a,]; sum := 0;
        for b to 5 do sum plusab arow[b] od;
        print (sum)
    od;
    print (newline);
    for b to 5 do
        ref[ ]int bcol = power[,b]; sum := 0;
        for a to 5 do sum plusab bcol[a] od;
        print (sum)
    od
end
```

3.3.6 Flexible Multiple Variables

All the multiple variables considered so far have referred to multiples with fixed bounds; i.e., the lower and upper bounds are constant values determined when their declarations are elaborated. We can also specify FLEXIBLE multiple variables which may refer to values with different bounds at different times after declaration. Programs which use flexible variables may be less efficient than others for reasons concerned with implementation;

nevertheless, for some applications flexibility is a powerful and valuable feature.

In the declaration of a flexible variable, the declarer begins with the symbol **flex**. For example, if a is declared as

    flex [*10*] **int** a

then a initially refers to a multiple with undefined elements and with bounds [*1*:*10*], but integer multiples with different bounds may later be assigned to it. The mode of a is **ref flex** [ ] **int**, and the mode of its value is [ ] **int**. Some more examples follow:

    flex [*3*] **int** b := (*20, 30, 40*);
    flex [*m*:*n*, *p*:*q*] **int** aa;
    flex [*1*:*0*] **int** c

The variable c initially refers to an empty multiple, which contains no elements at all.

The current bounds can be changed only by assignment of a complete multiple to the flexible name, as in

    c := (*20, 30, 40, 50*)

which changes the bounds of c to [*1*:*4*]. Whenever c is subscripted or trimmed the subscript or trimmer values must be in range, currently *1* to *4*. Assignment to the name of a submultiple of c is the same as in the preceding section, so that the statement

    $c[3:4]$:= (*60, 70*)

is valid with the current bounds of c, but the following are not:

    $c[5]$:= *60*
    $c[1:5]$:= (*10, 20, 30, 40, 50*)

The statement

    c := *10*

is valid and sets the bounds of c to [*1*:*1*] even though the mode of the right side appears to be **int** rather than [ ]**int**. The coercion involved here is called ROWING whereby a value of a mode M can be converted to a value of mode [ ]M. Rowing is also involved ([ ]**int** to [,]**int**) in

flex [*10,3*] **int** *bb* := *b*

which sets the bounds of *bb* to [*1:1,1:3*]. We can set the bounds of *c* to [*1:0*] again using an 'empty row display':

    c := ( )

Operators are available for determining the current values of bounds, regardless of whether the multiples are referred to by flexible names. Their characteristics are summarized in the following table:

Symbols		Priority	Modes
lwb	∟	*8*	(**int**, any row mode) **int**
lwb	∟	*10*	(any row mode) **int**
upb	⌐	*8*	(**int**, any row mode) **int**
upb	⌐	*10*	(any row mode) **int**

The left operand of the dyadic operators specifies the desired dimension; for example, the formula

    1 **upb** *bb*

yields the first upper bound of *bb*, and

    2 **lwb** *bb*

yields the second lower bound of *bb*. If the multiple is one-dimensional, or if the first dimension is the relevant one, the monadic operators may be used instead. Thus **upb** *c* is equivalent to *1* **upb** *c* and yields the current upper bound of *c*. These operators will become particularly useful in Chapter 5.

Phrases such as

    c := *bb*[*1*, **at** *2*]
    [*3*] **int** *d* := *c*
    [*2*] **int** *e* := *c*[:*3*]
    flex [*1:0*] **int** *f* := *c*
    [ ] **int** *g* = *c, h* = *c*[:*3*]

present no new problems, and the same considerations apply as before.

    Since flexibility is a property of names of multiples and not of the multiples themselves, the phrase

flex [ ] **int** $p = c$

is not a valid identity declaration, but the following one is:

ref flex [] **int** $p = c$

Finally, a slice of a flexible variable cannot be used as the right side of an identity declaration for a variable. Thus both of the following are illegal:

ref int $k = c[2]$
ref [ ] **int** $q = c[:3]$

3.3.7 Strings and Multiples (SCO)

Readers of these sections should have noticed many similarities between multiples and strings, such as the use of subscripts and trimmers, assignment to parts, and the existence of the rowing coercion and the operator **upb**. In fact, strings are actually character multiples; the declaration **string** s is equivalent to

flex $[1:0]$ **char** s

and string names have the mode **ref flex** [ ] **char**. To consolidate our knowledge of strings, then, we need only take note of a few special points and rules: (a) A string denotation may be regarded as an abbreviation for a row display; for example, $"abc""def"$ is equivalent to

$("a", "b", "c", " " " ", "d", "e", "f")$

(b) Since a string name generated by a non-initializing variable declaration initially refers to a multiple with no elements, it effectively has the null string as an initial value.
(c) The input of string values is handled differently from other multiples (see 2.3.4).
(d) The valid identity declaration

string $s = "abc"$

is equivalent to

[] **char** $s = ("a", "b", "c")$

(e) We have implicitly adopted the convention that strings always have a lower bound of 1.

Keeping these points in mind, the interested reader may verify that all constructs involving strings are consistent with the rules for flexible multiples in general.

There is nothing to prevent us from declaring other kinds of character multiple variables besides ones of mode **ref string**. For example,

[5] **char** *fs5*

generates a name which can refer to any multiple of five characters. If *fs5* is used as the left side of an assignation, the right side must yield a character multiple with bounds [*1:5*]. If it is used in an input statement, exactly five characters will be read, regardless of whether they can all be taken from the current line. In programs which process strings of constant length, it may be more efficient to declare them with fixed bounds instead of using **string**. The operators $+, *$, and **upb** will still be applicable.

The name generated by

[*50, 80*] **char** *page*

refers to *50* rows of *80* characters each. In the following program, it is used to store sets of fifty eighty-character lines, which are printed in reverse order:

```
begin
    [50, 80] char page;
    int n; read ((n, newline));
    to n do
      print (newpage);
      for i from 50 by − 1 to 1 do
        read (page[i,])
      od;
      for i to 50 do
        print ((page[i,], newline))
      od
    od
end
```

If the input lines have a variable number of characters, then *page* should be replaced by a string multiple variable:

[*50*] **string** *rs*

Now *rs*[*i*] yields the name of the *i*th row, and *rs*[*i*][*m:n*] yields the name of a substring of this row. If these slices would have to be elaborated several times for the same value of i, we could declare

ref string $rsi = rs[i]$

and use rsi and $rsi[m:n]$ instead. The preceding program can be rewritten as follows:

```
begin
    [50] string rs;
    int n; read ((n, newline));
    to n do
        print (newpage);
        for i from 50 by −1 to 1 do
            read ((rs[i], newline))
        od;
        for i to 50 do
            print ((rs[i], newline))
        od
    od
end
```

Exercises

1. Write a program which inputs a number n from one line of data and a string of n characters from the next line, and prints n lines, where the ith line consists of a string of 120 occurrences of the ith character input.
2. A set of input data consists of a number n on the first card followed by n cards containing text in the first 30 columns. Write a program to print the text in two columns, with 50 lines to a page and ten spaces between the columns. Assume for simplicity that n is a multiple of 100.

3.3.8 Matrix Processing (NUM)

Computations involving matrices are an important application for multiple values with the mode [,] **real**. The following sequence inputs two m-by-n matrices row by row and computes their sum:

```
int m, n; read ((m, n));
[m:n] real mat1, mat2, matsum;
read ((mat1, mat2));
for i to m do
    ref [ ] real rs = matsum[i,], r1 = mat1[i,],
                     r2 = mat2[i,];
```

```
    for j to n do
        rs[j] := r1[j] + r2[j]
    od
od
```

If the matix elements were ordered by column in the data, loop clauses would be required for their input. To output the sum matrix with one row to a line, we could write

for i **to** n **do** *print* ((*matsum*[i,], *newline*)) **od**

Multiplication of two matrices is defined when the number of columns n in the first matrix a is equal to the number of rows in the second matrix b. The element c_{ij} in the ith row and the jth column of the product matrix is defined as

$$c_{ij} = \sum_k a_{ik} \cdot b_{kj}$$

There is no difficulty in expressing this in Algol 68, bearing in mind the use of auxiliary variables for efficiency. As usual, the sum can be computed by means of a loop:

```
ref real cij = c[i,j] := 0;
for k to n do cij plusab a[i,k] * b[k,j] od
```

To compute all the elements of the product matrix, statements equivalent to these must be embedded in a nested loop where i and j will vary throughout their ranges of allowed values. In the following program, the three matrices are assumed to be square and small enough to be printed side by side:

```
begin
    int n; read (n);
    [n,n] real a, b, c; read ((a, b));
    for i to n do
        ref [ ] real arow = a[i,];
        for j to n do
            ref [ ] real bcol = b[,j];
            ref real cij = c[i,j] := 0;
            for k to n do
                cij plusab arow[k] * bcol[k]
            od
        od
    od;
```

```
    for i to n do
        print ((a[i,], b[i,], c[i,], newline))
    od
end
```

The next program outputs all the minors of a given *m*-by-*n* matrix. (The minor corresponding to a given element is the matrix obtained by deleting the row and column in which that element occurs.)

```
begin
    int m, n; read ((m, n));
    [m,n] real x; read (x);
    for i to m do
        for j to n do
            print ((newline, newline,
                "minor ̲ for ̲ x[",
                whole (i,0), ",", whole (j,0), "]:",
                newline, newline));
            for k to i − 1 do
                print ((x[k,:j − 1], x[k,j + 1:], newline))
            od;
            for k from i + 1 to m do
                print ((x[k,:j − 1], x[k,j + 1:], newline))
            od
        od
    od
end
```

All the matrices considered so far have been rectangular; i.e., all the rows have the same number of elements and all the columns have the same number of elements. This is the case even for the value of a flexible variable declared as

flex [*1:0, 1:0*] **real** *fv*

Sometimes it is desirable to have a means of representing non-rectangular matrices; for example, a symmetric square matrix would be more economically represented by a triangular object with one element in the first row, two in the second row, and so on. This can be achieved using a multiple where the names of the elements are flexible:

[*n*] **flex** [*1:0*] **real** *tr*

The rows can be filled in individually, as in

$tr[2] := (5, 12.6)$

or in groups, as in

$tr[1:3] := (5, (5, 12.6), (-2, 30, 0))$

The following statement inputs a complete set of values for *tr* row by row:

```
for i to n do
    [i] real row;
    read (row);
    tr[i] := row
od
```

It is impossible to declare an identifier for a column of *tr*. Thus, to input the values column by column, the element names must be used individually:

```
for i to n do
    [i] real row := skip;
    tr[i] := row
od;
for j to n do
    for i to n do read (tr[i] [j] od
od
```

The first loop is necessary because the only way of adjusting the size of the value of a flexible name is assignment of a complete multiple (which has undefined elements in this case); otherwise, the values of *j* in the slice $tr[i][j]$ would be out of range.

Exercises

1. Write statements to assign the minor corresponding to the element $x[4,5]$ in a *10*-by-*15* matrix *x* to a variable declared as

   [9, 14] **real** *minor*

2. Given that the result of applying an arithmetic operation to a matrix and a scalar number is obtained by performing the operation between the number and each element of the matrix, write a program which inputs an *m*-by-*n* matrix *a* and an *n*-by-*p* matrix *b*, finds their product matrix *c*, and outputs side by side the three matrices *c*, *c.2*, and *c.2* $-$ *1*.

Chapter 4
Conditional Elaboration

4.1 Decisions in Programs*

One of the most fundamental facts about programming is that the elaboration of parts of a program frequently must be conditional upon the particular circumstances which apply at the time. In other words, programs must be capable of making decisions from time to time to determine how to proceed. Decision-making generally involves comparing pairs of values or testing values for certain properties; this requires the use of a new mode which is introduced in 4.2.

Testing the nature or validity of input data is a simple example of the application of this concept. Suppose that a program is to input three numbers representing the dimensions of a box and to output the volume of the box. To be valid, each of the three numbers must be positive. The program can check that this is so and proceed with the volume calculation only on condition that the data is valid. Thus the program makes a decision either to perform a group of actions or to omit them. As a generalization of this notion, a program may perform one of two groups of actions depending on the result of its decision; one of the groups will be omitted in either case. In the volume calculation, for example, the program might either proceed with the calculation or print a message stating that the data is invalid. Constructs for this type of programming are introduced in 4.3.1, and some useful generalizations are described in 4.3.2.

Decision-making is also involved in the elaboration of loop clauses where the number of repetitions is not known at the beginning. A decision as to whether to terminate the loop must be made just before each prospective repetition. Such loops and examples of their use are the topics of 4.4.

4.2 The Boolean Mode

The symbol **bool** (for 'Boolean') is the indicant for another basic mode in the language. There are only two values of this mode, and their denotations are **true** and **false**. The most important use of these values is in the control of conditional elaboration, but we first consider their use in the various types of constructs covered in earlier chapters and introduce some new operators.

In the declarations

> **bool** $b1, b2, b3, b4 :=$ **true**;
> **bool** $t =$ **true**, $f =$ **false**

$b1, b2, b3$, and $b4$ are defined as variables of mode **ref bool**, $b4$ is initialized to the value **true**, and t and f are defined as Boolean constants.

The dyadic operators **and** and **or** are defined for Boolean operands and yield Boolean results; **and** yields **true** if both operands yield **true**, and **false** otherwise, while **or** yields **true** if either or both of the operands yield **true**. Since **and** has a higher priority than **or**, the value of

> $b4$ **or** f **and false**

is **true**, while

> $(b4$ **or** $f)$ **and false**

yields **false**. The monadic operator **not** yields the opposite value from that of its Boolean operand, so that

> **not** $b4$ **or** f

yields **false**.

To effect the comparison of numeric values, there are several dyadic operators yielding Boolean values given operands which yield integers, real numbers, or a combination of these. The operator $<$, for example, yields **true** if the value of the left operand is less than that of the right operand and **false** otherwise. Similarly, we have $>$ (greater than), $\leq$ (less than or equal to), $\geq$ (greater than or equal to), $=$ (equal to), and $\neq$ (not equal to). The last two of these have a lower priority than the others, but they all have lower priority than the dyadic arithmetic operators ($+, *$, etc.) and higher priority than the dyadic Boolean operators (**and, or**). (See the table at the end of this section.) Thus all of the following formulas yield **true**:

> $5 > 4$ **and** $6.3 \neq 9.2$
> $0 = 1$ **or** $10 + 7 \leq 17$
> t **and not** $(-5 + 2 = 3$ **or** $f)$

The operators $=$ and $\neq$ are also defined when both operands are Boolean, so that both of the following yield **true**:

$$b4 = (10 > 9)$$
$$(b4 = b4) \neq (b4 = f)$$

Note, however, that there is never any need to use these with an operand consisting of a Boolean denotation, because the following formulas are all equivalent to either $b1$ or **not** $b1$:

$b1 =$ **true**	**true** $= b1$
$b1 \neq$ **true**	**true** $\neq b1$
$b1 =$ **false**	**false** $= b1$
$b1 \neq$ **false**	**false** $\neq b1$

The monadic operator **odd** yields **true** if its integer operand is odd, and **false** if it is even, so that

odd 29

yields **true**, while

odd $(5 + 7)$

yields **false**. The operator **abs** transforms a Boolean value into an integer: 1 for **true** and 0 for **false**. Thus the value of

$50 +$ **abs** $(i > 1) * 25$

will be either 50 or 75, depending on whether the value of i is greater than 1.

It is of course possible to have Boolean multiples:

flex $[1:0]$ **bool** bs
$[0:n, 0:n]$ **bool** rel

The variable bs could be used for a variable-length string of bit values, and rel might represent an algebraic relation on a set of $n + 1$ elements.

The following statements assign Boolean values to **ref bool** names:

$b1 := i < 5$ **or odd upb** bs
$b2 := rel[3,4] := i = 3$

As for transput, the external representations for **true** and **false** depend upon the environment but will be written here as **T** and **F**, respectively. The actual representations are given by the environment enquiries *flip* and *flop*, both of mode **char**. When a **ref bool** name is used in a call of *read*, the first nonblank character in the input data must be T or F. On output, T or F is printed with no preceding space. As with numeric values, new lines and pages are begun automatically when necessary. Boolean multiples are straightened in the usual way, so that

   print (((**true**, **true**), (**false**, **false**)))

will result in the output

   TTFF

To conclude this section, here is a summary of the operators involving Boolean values which have been introduced so far:

Symbols			Priority	Modes
or	∨		*2*	**(bool, bool) bool**
and	∧		*3*	**(bool, bool) bool**
=	**eq**		*4*	**(bool, bool) bool**
				(int, int) bool
				(real, real) bool
				(real, int) bool
				(int, real) bool
≠	/ =	**ne**	*4*	as for =
<	**lt**		*5*	**(int, int) bool**
				(real, real) bool
				(real, int) bool
				(int, real) bool
≤	< =	**le**	*5*	as for <
≥	> =	**ge**	*5*	as for <
>	**gt**		*5*	as for <
abs			*10*	**(bool) int**
odd			*10*	**(int) bool**
not	¬	~	*10*	**(bool) bool**

Exercises

1. If the values of $b1$, $b2$, and i are **true**, **false**, and 5, respectively, determine the values yielded by each of the following formulas:

   (a) $b1$ **and not** $b2$ **and** $i = 5$
   (b) **odd abs** ($i = 5 = b1$)
   (c) **abs odd** i + **abs** ($i \le 5$) + **abs** i

2. Point out the errors in each of the following:

   (a) $4 < 5 < 6$
   (b) $i = 5$ **or** 6
   (c) **not** $5 \geq 6$

4.3 Conditional Clauses

4.3.1 Simple Conditionals

A CONDITIONAL CLAUSE is a type of unit in which the elaboration of one or more parts is conditional on the Boolean result of the elaboration of another part. There are two basic forms, the simpler of which is

if Boolean-series **then** series **fi**

The elaboration of the construct begins with the Boolean series; if it yields **true**, the other series is then elaborated; otherwise, nothing further is done.
   The conditional statement

if $a = b$ **then** $c := d + e$ **fi**

specifies that the assignment is to be carried out if the values of a and b are equal. As a more complicated example, consider

if int i; *read* (i); **odd** i
then int j; *read* (j); *print* $(i + j)$
fi

The range of i is the entire clause, and the range of j is the series following the symbol **then**. The effect of the statement is to input an integer and, if it is odd, to input a second integer and output the sum of the two.
   The second basic form of conditional is

if Boolean-series **then** series **else** series **fi**

The third series also constitutes the range of any identifiers declared in it. The Boolean series is elaborated first; if it yields **true**, the second series is elaborated, and if it yields **false**, the third series is elaborated. As an example, if p has the mode **bool** or **ref bool**, we could have

if p **then** a **plusab** b **else int** z; *read* (z); c **timesab** z **fi**

The set of indicants **if**, **then**, **else**, and **fi** may be replaced by the symbols $(, |, |$, and $)$, respectively. Thus the following statements are equivalent to those given above:

$(a = b | c := d + e)$
(**int** i; $read(i)$; **odd** i | **int** j; $read(j)$; $print(i + j)$)
$(p | a$ **plusab** b | **int** z; $read (z)$; c **timesab** $z)$

Conditional clauses can be expressions as well as statements. For example,

$(i > 5 | x + y | x - y)$

yields the value of either $x + y$ or $x - y$ depending on the value of i. The clause may form part of a larger unit in the same way as a closed clause. For example,

$i := (i = 1 | x | y) + 5$

is equivalent to

if $i = 1$ **then** $i := x + 5$ **else** $i := y + 5$ **fi**

If a conditional without an **else** part is used as an expression, its value will be undefined when the Boolean series yields **false** (because **else skip** is assumed when there is no **else** part).

The mode yielded by a conditional expression must always be determinable in advance of its elaboration. The question of what happens when one part apparently yields an integer and the other a real number, for example, leads us into one of the finer points of the language. Suppose that i is an integer variable and x is a real variable. Then we know that in

$x := i$

the value of i will be widened, but in

$x := 6.3 + i$

it will not. (The version of $+$ between a **real** and an **int** will be used, yielding a **real**.) Similarly, widening of either i or 5 will take place in

$x := (i = 1 | i | 5)$

and, perhaps, of i in

$$x := (i\ =\ 1\,|\,6.3\,|\,i)$$

but not in

$$x := 6.3\ +\ (i\ =\ 1\,|\,i\,|\,5)$$

Now by virtue of a phenomenon called BALANCING, which permits coercions to occur where they otherwise could not, widening of i's value also takes place in either of the following:

$$x := 6.3\ +\ (i\ =\ 1\,|\,i\,|\,6.3)$$
$$x := 6.3\ +\ (i\ =\ 1\,|\,6.3\,|\,i)$$

In other words, if one of the parts of the conditional is real-valued, balancing permits the other to be widened if necessary, and the relevant version of + is the one defined for two real operands.

Conditional clauses are used for many different purposes. The following conditional statement contains a Boolean conditional expression:

if $(i\ =\ 0\,|\,x < y\,|$ **false**) **then** *print* $(x\ +\ y)$ **fi**

This differs from

if $i\ =\ 0$ **and** $x < y$ **then** *print* $(x\ +\ y)$ **fi**

in that x and y will never be compared if the value of i is 0. In the assignation

$$(i\ =\ 0\,|\,i\,|\,j) := 15$$

the left side consists of a conditional expression yielding an integer name, which is not dereferenced. The statement is equivalent to

if $i\ =\ 0$ **then** $i := 15$ **else** $j := 15$ **fi**

As still another example, the slice

$$(i\ =\ 0\,|\,aa\,|\,bb)\ [1,\,2\!:\!5]$$

is equivalent to either $aa[1,2\!:\!5]$ or $bb[1,2\!:\!5]$. In general, a conditional expression yielding a value of some mode M, possibly with the aid of coercions and balancing, may appear in the same contexts as any other expression of mode M.

Here now is a simple, self-explanatory program containing a conditional clause:

```
( int length, width, height;
  read ((length, width, height));
  if length ≤ 0 or width ≤ 0 or height ≤ 0
  then print ("error ‒ in ‒ data")
  else int volume  =  length * width * height;
     print (("volume ‒ = ", volume, newline,
         "cost ‒‒‒", fixed(15 * volume, 7, 2)))
  fi )
```

Exercises

1. Describe the elaboration of each of the following units:

   (a) if i = 0 or j = 0 then x := y; y plusab z fi
   (b) if odd i then i plusab 1 else i minusab 1 fi
   (c) if b1 then 5 else int k; read(k); k fi
   (d) upb if b1 then a := (1, 2, 3, 4, 5) else b := ( ) fi
   (e) if if b1 then b2 else false fi then print(x) fi

2. Re-express each of the above in abbreviated notation.
3. Write a program which inputs three numbers, tests whether they are in ascending order, and outputs a message stating the result of the test.

4.3.2 Nested Conditionals and Case Clauses

The series within a conditional clause may themselves contain conditional clauses, as in the following example (which has the same effect as an example given near the end of the preceding section):

```
if i  =  0
then if x < y then print (x + y) fi
fi
```

An inner conditional may contain an else part:

```
if i  =  0
then if x < y then print (x + y) else read ( (x, y) ) fi
fi
```

Note that this differs from

```
if i  =  0 and x < y
then print (x + y) else read ( (x, y) ) fi
```

not only in that x and y are not compared when $i \neq 0$, but also in that the **else** part is not elaborated when $i \neq 0$.

There is an abbreviated notation for the nesting of conditionals within **else** parts. Whenever an **else** part consists of another conditional, the symbols **else if** may be replaced by **elif** and the **fi** of the inner clause omitted; i.e., a construction of the form **else if** ... **fi fi** may be shortened to **elif** ... **fi**. Thus

> **if** $i = 0$ **then** *print* $(x + y)$
> **elif** $x < y$ **then** *read* $((x, y))$
> **fi**

is equivalent to

> **if** $i = 0$ **then** *print* $(x + y)$
> **else if** $x < y$ **then** *read* $((x, y))$ **fi**
> **fi**

The alternative representation for **elif** is | :, so that

> $(\quad i = 0 \mid print (x + y)$
> $\mid : x < y \mid read ((x, y))$
> $\mid : v = w \mid x$ **plusab** y
> $\qquad\qquad \mid v$ **plusab** $w \qquad)$

is the most abbreviated form of

> **if** $i = 0$
> **then** *print* $(x + y)$
> **else if** $x < y$
>   **then** *read* $((x, y))$
>   **else if** $v = w$
>   **then** x **plusab** y
>   **else** v **plusab** w
>   **fi**
>   **fi**
> **fi**

If the expression

> $(\quad i = 1 \mid 20$
> $\mid : i = 2 \mid 53$

```
| : i  =  3 | 75
| : i  =  4 | 112.5
| : i  =  5 | 260
          | 0    )
```

were used as an operand, the six alternatives would be balanced: the fact that one would yield a real value (*112.5*) means that any of the others could be coerced to **real**.

The effect of a conditional clause containing a long sequence of **elif** parts is often achieved more efficiently by a CASE CLAUSE, which has the general form

> **case** integer-series
> **in**   two-or-more-units-separated-by-commas
> **out** series
> **esac**

The range of any identifiers declared in the **case** part is the entire clause, and the **out** part constitutes an inner range. The **case** part is elaborated first, and if its value V is between *1* and the number of units in the **in** part, then unit number V therein is elaborated; otherwise, the series in the **out** part is elaborated. The **out** part may be omitted, in which case **out skip** is assumed. Case clauses can be used in the same contexts as conditionals, and the alternatives in a case expression may be balanced. The symbols **case, in, out**, and **esac** may be replaced by (, | , | , and), respectively. Thus the following case expression is equivalent to the conditional given previously:

> (*i* | *20, 53, 75, 112.5, 260* | *0*)

As a more complicated example, consider the following conditional statement:

> **if** $n \geq 10$ **and** $n < 20$ **then** *print* (*a*)
> **elif** $n \geq 30$ **and** $n < 40$ **then** $c := a; a := $ b
> **elif** $n \geq 40$ **and** $n < 50$ **then** *print* (*b*)
> **fi**

This may be replaced by the case statement

> **case** $n \div 10$
> **in** *print* (*a*),
>   **skip**,
>   ($c := a; a := b$),

     print (*b*)
  esac

If an **out** part consists of another case clause, the symbols **out case** may be replaced by **ouse** and the **esac** of the inner clause omitted; i.e., **out case** ... **esac esac** may be shortened to **ouse** ... **esac**. The alternative representation for **ouse** is | :.

Exercises

1. Rewrite the following expression so as to remove as many **fi** symbols as possible:

   if *a* **then** *b* **else if** *c* **then if** *d* **then** *e* **fi else** *f* **fi fi**

Rewrite it again in its most abbreviated form.

2. Rewrite the following expression in its least abbreviated form:

   (*a* | (*b* | *c* |: *d* | *e* |: *f* | *g*))

3. Rewrite the following as a case clause:

   if $n = -2$ **then** *a* **elif** $n = -1$ **then** *b* **elif** $n = 0$
   then *c* **elif** $n = 1$ **then** *d* **else** *e* **fi**

4.3.3. Additional Non-numeric Facilities (SCO)

The following table is a summary of some additional operators for the comparison of character and string values:

Symbols	Priority	Modes
= **eq**	*4*	(**char** , **char**) **bool**
		(**string, string**) **bool**
		(**string, char**) **bool**
		(**char, string**) **bool**
≠ /= **ne**	*4*	as for =
< **lt**	*5*	as for =
≤ < = **le**	*5*	as for =
≥ > = **ge**	*5*	as for =
> **gt**	*5*	as for =

If *c1* and *c2* yield character values, then *c1* < *c2* is true if and only if

   abs *c1* < **abs** *c2*

The value yielded is thus dependent on the environment, but it will frequently be the case that all of the following are true:

$"\dot{-}" < "a"$	$"0" < "1"$
$"a" < "b"$	$"1" < "2"$
$"b" < "c"$	$"2" < "3"$
$\vdots$	$\vdots$
$"y" < "z"$	$"8" < "9"$

The other operators with character operands have the obvious corresponding meanings.

For string operands, $s1 < s2$ is true either if the first character C in $s1$ that differs from the corresponding character D in $s2$ is such that $C < D$, or if $s1 = s2[:i]$, where $i <$ **upb** $s2$. If one operand is a character, it is treated as a string of length one. Thus all of the following are true, given the truth of the formulas in the previous paragraph:

$"abc" = "abc"$	$"abc" \le "abc"$
$"a" < "abc"$	$"abc" \ge "a"$
$"a" \ne "abc"$	$"ab\dot{-}" < "aba"$
$"\ " < "a"$	$"aa" < "ba"$

These operators will work for any operands yielding one-dimensional character multiples and not just ones of mode **string**.

The following program inputs three words of ten characters each and outputs them in alphabetical order:

```
begin
  [10] char s1, s2, s3;
  read ( (s1, s2, s3) );
  if s1 < s2
  then if s2 < s3
    then print ( (s1, s2, s3) )
    elif s1 < s3
    then print ( (s1, s3, s2) )
    else print ( (s3, s1, s2) )
    fi
  elif s1 < s3
    then print ( (s2, s1, s3) )
    elif s2 < s3
    then print ( (s2, s3, s1) )
```

```
    else print ( (s3, s2, s1) )
  fi
end
```

4.4 Conditional Loops

4.4.1 The while Construction

Conditional clauses may contain loop clauses, as in

```
if x < y
then s := 0;
  for i to 1 upb aa do
    ref [ ] int row  =  aa [i,];
    for j to 2 upb aa do s plusab row [j] od
  od ;
  s2 := s * s
else s := s2 := 1
fi
```

On the other hand, loop clauses may contain conditionals. In the following sequence, successive elements of a one-dimensional multiple a are printed until a given value p is reached:

```
bool not found := true;
for i to upb a do
  if not found
  then print (a[i]);
    if a[i]  =  p then not found := false fi
  fi
od
```

In effect, we have a loop such that the exact number of repetitions is not known, even after its elaboration has begun; all that is known about the number of meaningful repetitions is an upper limit given by the value of **upb** a. Any loop with these properties could be set up in this way with the aid of a Boolean variable and a conditional statement, but it is more convenient and more efficient to use a **while** construction in the loop clause:

```
bool not found := true
for i to upb a while not found do
  print (a[i]);
  if a[i]  =  p then not found := false fi
od
```

The most general form of loop clause is

for I **from** J **by** K **to** L **while** P **do** S **od**

where I, J, K, L, and S are as described in 3.2.1. and P is a series yielding a Boolean value. For each repetition, the value of the constant I is determined as before, but then P is elaborated. If it yields **true**, the repetition proceeds; otherwise, the loop is terminated. All the loops considered previously implicitly contained the construction **while true**, so that it was always the value of L which, together with J and K, determined the number of repetitions. In the general case, or in a loop of the form

to L **while** P **do** S **od**

L determines only an upper limit on the number of repetitions; the loop may be terminated by P yielding **false** before any prospective repetition.

The part of the clause between the symbols **while** and **od** constitutes a range surrounding the range formed by the **do** part. Moreover, the identifier in the **for** part, although local to the loop clause and not available to the **from, by,** and **to** parts, is global to both these ranges. The following is a more efficient version of the previous example:

for i **to upb** a **while** $a[i] \neq p$ **do** *print* (a[i]) **od**;
print (p)

Since a **while** part is elaborated once before every repetition, it should not involve computations which must always give the same result. For example,

for i **to upb** a **while** $c < d$ **and** $e < f$ **and** $a[i] \neq p$
    do *print* ($a[i]$) **od**

is inefficient and could be replaced by

if $c < d$ **and** $e < f$
then for i **to upb** a **while** $a[i] \neq p$
    do *print* ($a[i]$) **od**
fi

Some loops are such that not even an upper limit on the number of repetitions is known when they are begun. The **while** construction is essential in such cases, since the **to** part is then usually omitted. For example, here is a program which forms the sum of an unknown number of input values terminated in the data by the value 0:

```
( int x, sum := 0; read (x);
  while x ≠ 0 do sum plusab x; read (x) od;
  print (sum) )
```

As a nontrivial example of the use of **while**, consider the problem of sorting the *n* elements of an integer multiple into ascending order using the 'bubble' method. In this algorithm, successive pairs of elements (first and second, second and third, etc.) are compared and interchanged if necessary. After all adjacent pairs of the *n* elements have been so treated, the process is repeated for only the first *n-1* elements, and again for the first *n-2* elements, and so on until either no interchanges occur during a pass, or the pass involving only the first two elements is completed.

The interchange of two successive elements can be accomplished with the statements

$$temp := a[i]; a[i] := a[i + 1]; a[i + 1] := temp$$

During the first pass, the value of *i* will range from *1* to *n-1*, during the second pass from *1* to *n-2*, and so on. Thus all its values in all passes can be specified by a nested loop which begins with

```
for j from n − 1 by − 1 to 1 do
  for i to j do
```

However, it may not be necessary to carry out all *n-1* passes, since this is only an upper limit. Thus we add a **while** part to the outer loop clause, with a Boolean variable *active* to indicate whether sorting is complete. Its value will be set to **false** just before each pass and reset to **true** whenever an interchange takes place. The complete program follows:

```
begin
  int temp, n; read (n);
  [n] int a; read (a);
  bool active := true;
  for j from n − 1 by − 1 to 1 while active do
    active := false;
    for i to j do
      ref int ai = a[i], ai1 = a[i + 1];
      if ai > ai1
      then temp := ai;
        ai := ai1;
        ai1 := temp;
        active := true
```

```
          fi
        od
      od;
       print (a)
    end
```

The conditional loop is the most powerful control device introduced so far and should be used with care. By including a **while** part and omitting a **to** part, it is possible to write 'infinite' loops, which never reach normal termination:

```
    int s := 1;
    while s > 0 do s plusab 1 od
```

An infinite loop can wastefully use up all the remaining time allocated to the job, and in realistic cases debugging is often difficult because of a lack of informative output. It is therefore best to check carefully that no loop can be repeated indefinitely when writing the program in the first place.

It is in fact possible to omit both the **to** part and the **while** part; with the facilities we have so far, such loops are necessarily infinite. However, they are sometimes useful in conjunction with the special identifier *stop*, the true nature of which is explained in 8.1. It may be regarded as a special unit which causes immediate termination of the entire program. As a trivial example, the following program prints all the input data, which is terminated by the value 0:

```
    ( int x;
      do read (x);
        if x = 0 then stop fi
        print (x)
      od )
```

Exercises

1. Given the declaration

   [*m, n*] **int** *aa*

   write statements to print successive elements of *aa* until a value *p* is encountered.
2. Rewrite these statements so that the program is immediately terminated if and when *p* is encountered.
3. Write a program which reads and finds the average of a set of integers terminated by, but not including, the value 0.

4.4.2 Text Processing (SCO)

For our purposes, 'text' consists of many lines of data to be interpreted as character strings, possibly but not necessarily expressed in a natural language. Many areas of non-numeric programming involve text processing, including compiler writing and statistical or stylistic analysis of literature. To illustrate some of the relevant programming techniques, we consider the problem of printing English text in right-justified format; i.e., given the unformatted data

```
This text is to be printed in right-justified
format. The
program must compose
each line of some fixed length in such a way that
the last character is not a blank.
It will have to
pad the breaks between words with blanks
when necessary.
```

the output might appear as follows:

```
This text is to be printed   in
right-justified  format.   The
program must compose each line
of some fixed length in such a
way that the last character is
not a blank. It will  have  to
pad the breaks  between  words
with blanks when necessary.
```

Let us assume that the input lines are of varying length and do not have trailing blanks. Then one input line may correspond to several output lines, and one output line may be taken from several input lines. To avoid reading all the text at once, which would probably require too much memory, a string variable *buffer* will be used to hold those input lines from which the next output line is to be composed. The first part of *buffer* will generally consist of a tail of a preceding input line which has not yet been completely processed. If *outlen* is an integer constant representing the length of the output lines and *inline* is a string variable referring to an input line, the following statement will build *buffer* up to a sufficient length:

> **while upb** *buffer* < *outlen* **do**
>   *read* ((*inline*, *newline*));
>   *buffer* **plusab** *blank* + *inline*

od

The blank is inserted so that the last word of an input line will be separated from the first word of the next input line in the printout.

We have not yet allowed for reaching the end of the data, which we shall assume is marked by a line beginning with the character ← All that then remains is to print the value of *buffer*, since the last output line should not be right-justified.

If the last line has not yet been reached, we must extract the longest head (*chunk*) of *buffer* which can be padded with blanks to form an output line. This can be done by scanning the string from right to left beginning at position *outline* + *1* until a blank is found. The value of *chunk* is the substring to the left of this blank (and any others immediately to its left), and the number (*diff*) of blanks with which it must be padded is equal to the number of characters scanned. The following statements compute these values and reset the value of *buffer*, skipping the blank since we do not want it to appear at the beginning of a subsequent output line:

```
diff := 0;
for i from outlen + 1 by −1 to 1
   while buffer[i] ≠ blank
   do diff plusab 1 od;
j := outlen − diff;
for i from j by −1 to 1
   while buffer[i] = blank
   do diff plusab 1 od;
chunk := buffer [:outlen − diff];
buffer := buffer [j + 2:]
```

Now we must locate the sequences of one or more blanks within *chunk* where padding can take place. Each of these positions within *chunk* will be used not just once but twice in composing the output line. Thus it is best to store them in a multiple value *breaks* of sufficient size to handle the largest possible number of break positions. Any blanks which appear at the beginning of the string do not count as a break. The following statements fill in the relevant elements of *breaks* and assign their number to *nb*:

```
nb := 0; j := 1;
while chunk[j] = blank do j plusab 1 od;
while j < upb chunk do
   j plusab 1;
   if chunk[j] = blank
   then nb plusab 1; breaks[nb] := j;
      while chunk[j] = blank do j plusab 1 od
```

fi
od

Note that j does not appear in a **for** part in the first loop clause because its value is required upon completion, while in the second loop its value is changed in an unpredictable manner in the **do** part.

There are *diff* blanks to be inserted and *nb* places where they can be put. We want the padding to be balanced, so that if a total of eight blanks are to be inserted in three places, for example, the insertions should consist of two strings of three blanks each and one string of two blanks. A little thought will confirm that in general $diff \div nb + 1$ blanks should be inserted at *diff* **mod** *nb* places, and $diff \div nb$ blanks at the remaining places. Thus it is convenient to build two strings of blanks, *short* and *long*, where *long* contains one more character than *short*:

$$long := spaces\ [1 : diff \div nb + 1];$$
$$short := long\ [2:];$$
$$nshort := nb - diff\ \textbf{mod}\ nb$$

The value of *nshort* is the number of places where *short* is to be inserted; *spaces* is assumed to represent a sufficiently long string of blanks.

The output line can be built up by taking successive parts of *chunk* between breaks and interspersing them with instances of *long* or *short*. To simplify the situation for the first and last parts of *chunk*, it is convenient to extend the multiple *breaks* so that the respective values of *breaks*[0] and *breaks* [$nb + 1$] are the position numbers of the first and last characters of *chunk*. Then the following statements print the output line:

```
for i to nshort do print
    ((chunk[breaks[i−1] : breaks[i]−1], short)) od;
print (chunk[breaks[nshort] : breaks[nshort + 1]]);
for i from nshort + 1 to nb do print
    ((long, chunk[breaks[i]+1 : breaks[i + 1]])) od
```

It is important to note that this will work for the special cases where no insertions of *long* are carried out (*nshort* = *nb*), where *short* refers to the empty string, and where both of these conditions hold.

The entire process is repeated until the data is exhausted. With a few minor modifications of the parts given above, the complete program may be written as follows:

```
begin
    string buffer, inline, chunk, long, short;
```

```
int outlen  =   30; char stopper  =   "←";
string spaces  =  outlen ∗ blank;
int diff, chunklen, nb, j, nshort;
[0:outlen÷2+1] int breaks; breaks[0] := 1;
do while upb buffer ≤ outlen
  do read ((inline, newline));
    if inline[1]  =  stopper
    then print (buffer); stop
    else buffer plusab blank  +  inline
    fi
  od;

  diff := 0;
  for i from outlen  +  1 by  −1 to 1 while buffer[i] ≠ blank
    do diff plusab 1 od;
  j := outlen  −  diff;
  for i from j by  −1 to 1 while buffer[i]  =  blank
    do diff plusab 1 od;
  chunklen := outlen  −  diff;
  chunk := buffer[:chunklen];
  buffer := buffer[j  +  2:];
  nb := 0; j := 1;
  while chunk[j]  =  blank do j plusab 1 od;
  while j < chunklen do
    j plusab 1;
    if chunk[j]  =  blank
    then nb plusab 1; breaks[nb] := j;
      while chunk[j]  =  blank do j plusab 1 od
    fi
  od;

  breaks[nb  +  1] := chunklen;
  long := spaces[1:diff÷nb  +  1];
  short := long[2:];
  nshort := nb  −  diff mod nb;
  for i to nshort do print
    ((chunk[breaks[i  −  1] : breaks[i]  −  1], short)) od;
  print (chunk[breaks[nshort]: breaks[nshort  +  1]]);
  for i from nshort  +  1 to nb do print
    ((long, chunk[breaks[i]+1: breaks[i  +  1]])) od;
  print (newline)
  od
end
```

To keep the program relatively short, it has been assumed that the input data will be 'reasonable'. The reader may be able to think of some contingencies where the program will fail or produce unsatisfactory output. A similar remark applies to efficiency; in particular, some of the strings could be replaced by fixed-length character multiples at the expense of more complexity and less understandability.

Exercises

1. Write a program to read input lines of variable length and print them on separate lines with all blanks removed. The end of the input data is marked by a ← in the first column.
2. Rewrite the above program so that each output string is centred on its line, which has 120 characters in all.

4.4.3 Numerical Approximation (NUM)

Conditional loops are essential for a wide variety of numerical calculations involving iterative approximation. In many of these problems, the fact that real numbers do not in general have exact computer representations is important, since repeated arithmetic operations give rise to roundoff errors which may build up and give completely erroneous results. These considerations, which come under the heading of numerical analysis, are largely outside the scope of this book. Similarly, the choice of which algorithm or 'numerical method' to use in writing a program for certain problems is an important question which can scarcely be touched on here.

As a first example, suppose that the predefined procedure *exp* is not available, and that we decide to compute e^x using the convergent infinite series

$$e^x = 1 + x + \frac{x^2}{2!} + \frac{x^3}{3!} + \ldots$$

After a time, the magnitudes of the terms will become negligible; let us assume that we can ignore the terms smaller than the environment enquiry *small real*. The number of relevant terms then depends on the value of x, so that a loop clause with a **while** part is needed in order to accumulate the sum. The most obvious strategy is to compute each term separately and add it to the sum already accumulated. We can obtain a much more efficient method, however, by noting that the nth term (where the terms are numbered from *0*) can be obtained by multiplying the previous term by x / n. Thus the following sequence assigns the required value to *expx*:

real *expx* := *0*, *term* := *1*;

```
for n while abs term > small real do
    expx plusab term;
    term timesab x / n
od
```

Some nonlinear equations can be solved by a process of computing better and better approximations to a root. For example, the nth root x of a number a can be found by iterating the equation

$$x = \frac{1}{n}\left((n - 1)x + \frac{a}{x^{n-1}}\right)$$

i.e., an initial approximation for x (perhaps a itself) is substituted in the right-hand expression to obtain a second approximation, which is in turn used to obtain a third approximation, and so on. The process stops when the difference between a pair of successive approximations is sufficiently small for the accuracy desired. In the following sequence, $xnew$ is used to hold the most recent approximation and contains the result at the end:

```
int nless1 = n − 1;
real xold := 0, xnew := a,
while abs (xold − xnew) > small real do
    xold := xnew;
    xnew := (nless1 * xold + a / xold ↑ nless1) / n
od
```

Now consider the problem of solving a set of n simultaneous linear equations of the form

$$\begin{aligned}
a_{11}x_1 + a_{12}x_2 + \ldots + a_{1n}x_n &= b_1 \\
a_{21}x_1 + a_{22}x_2 + \ldots + a_{2n}x_n &= b_2 \\
\vdots \qquad\quad \vdots \qquad\qquad\quad \vdots \qquad\quad \vdots \\
a_{n1}x_1 + a_{n2}x_2 + \ldots + a_{nn}x_n &= b_n
\end{aligned}$$

Given the values of the a's and b's as data, it is required to find the values of the n x's. In one method, called Jacobi's method, the equations are first rewritten in the form

$$x_1 = \frac{1}{a_{11}}(b_1 - a_{12}x_2 - a_{13}x_3 - \ldots - a_{1n}x_n)$$

$$x_2 = \frac{1}{a_{22}}(-a_{21}x_1 + b_2 - a_{23}x_3 - \dots - a_{2n}x_n)$$

$$\cdot \quad \cdot$$
$$\cdot \quad \cdot$$
$$\cdot \quad \cdot$$

$$x_n = \frac{1}{a_{nn}}(-a_{n1}x_1 - a_{n2}x_2 - a_{n3}x_3 - \dots + b_n)$$

Now, given some initial approximations for the x's, these equations are iterated to produce new approximations, until the difference between successive approximations of each x is no larger than some small value. In the following program, the multiple *xnew* contains the latest approximations (initially all *0*), and the Boolean variable *active* is used to control the number of iterations:

```
begin
    int n; read (n);
    [n,n] real a; [n] real b, xold, xnew;
    for i to n do
        read ((a[i,], b[i]));
        xnew[i] := 0 od;
    bool active := true;
    while active do
        for i to n do xold[i] := xnew[i] od;
        active := false;
        for i to n do
            ref real xnewi = xnew[i] := b[i];
            ref [ ] real arow = a[i,];
            for j to i − 1 do
                xnewi minusab arow[j] * xold[j] od;
            for j from i + 1 to n do
                xnewi minusab arow[j] * xold[j] od;
            xnewi divab arow[i];
            if abs (xnewi − xold[i] > small real then
                active := true fi
        od
    od;
    print (xnew)
end
```

Jacobi's method is a useful one when the diagonal coefficients a_{11}, a_{22}, $\dots$, a_{nn} are large compared with the other coefficients, especially when n is large and most of the coefficients are zero.

Exercises

1. Given the infinite series

$$\tanh^{-1} x = x + \frac{x^3}{3} + \frac{x^5}{5} + \ \ldots$$

   write statements to assign the inverse hyperbolic tangent of x to *arc tanh*.
2. Using an initial approximation of *0.5*, write a 'one-shot' program to solve the equation

   $$x = \cos x$$

   by iterative approximation.
3. Write a program to solve a set of linear equations by the Gauss-Seidel method. This is similar to Jacobi's method except that the latest approximation to each x is used at all times; for example, in calculating the second approximation to x_2, the second rather than the first approximation to x_1 is used.

Chapter 5
Routines

5.1 The Concept of Program Modularity*

The segmentation of large programs into smaller, sometimes self-contained sections is another fundamental programming concept, and one which is important for several different reasons. First, it is often the case that the same or nearly the same computations, perhaps requiring a considerable number of statements, must be repeated at different places in a program. To reduce coding effort and the size of the compiled program, it is then advisable to program the computation as a separate object called a ROUTINE and invoke it at each place where it is required. When an invocation is elaborated, the effect is the same as elaborating the routine at that point in the program.

A program may contain many routines, each of which performs some well-defined task. Conversely, a routine may be usefully invoked by two or more separate programs; the implementation may then permit the routine to be compiled separately from any program which will later make use of it. As far as the coding process is concerned, the routines may be mutually independent; this is important in very large programs where different routines may be written by different programmers.

Once a routine has been written and debugged, it may be thought of as a basic facility which can be used as a component of further computations, much as a mathematician uses a previously proved theorem as if it were an axiom when proving another theorem. In effect, routines provide the programmer with a higher level of language. A part of a program written at this higher level (i.e., containing invocations of the routines) will be shorter, easier to write, and easier to understand than would otherwise be the case.

When a program or part of a program becomes too long to be easily comprehensible (over 50 lines, say), it is often advisable to break it up into routines. As an idealized example, a 100-line program might be replaced by two 50-line routines and an invocation of each. Each routine could itself be divided into routines, and so on, and this concept leads to a method of programming known as TOP-DOWN programming. One of the features of this method is that the highest-level sections are written before the routines which they invoke, taking into account what the routines will do but not how they will do it. The merits and techniques of top-down programming are somewhat beyond our scope, but the concept should be borne in mind when writing programs which are larger and more complex than the examples in this book.

In Algol 68, routines are defined by procedure declarations, described in 5.2, and operation declarations, described in 5.3.

5.2 Procedures

We use the term PROCEDURE when speaking of routines which are defined and elaborated in special ways described in these sections. A routine has one of an indefinite number of modes, each of which begins with the symbol **proc**, and is represented in a program by a unit called a ROUTINE TEXT.

5.2.1 Procedures Without Parameters

For the type of procedure considered in this section, a routine text has the general form

    declarer : unit

The declarer, which may be **void**, specifies the mode of the value, if any, which is delivered by the procedure, i.e., yielded by an invocation of the procedure. The unit specifies the computations to be carried out when the procedure is invoked; it is often a closed clause or conditional clause containing declarations of local identifiers, so that a significant amount of work may be carried out. The value of the unit must have the mode specified by the declarer; all coercions are applicable in this context.

The following phrase is an identity declaration for a simple procedure with the identifier xyz:

$$\textbf{proc void } xyz \;=\; \textbf{void} : (x := 1; y := 2; z := 3)$$

This is analogous to other identity declarations, and the right side could be any unit yielding a routine of mode **proc void**, such as a previously declared **proc void** identifier. In cases such as the above, however, where the right side is a routine text, the following alternative form may be used:

    proc identifier = routine-text

Thus xyz is more concisely declared by

proc xyz = **void** : $(x := 1; y := 2; z := 3)$

This procedure makes use of three variables x, y, and z, which are global to the unit

$(x := 1; y := 2; z := 3)$

The crucial point is that this unit is elaborated not when the declaration is elaborated, but only when the procedure is later invoked. In the simplest case, an invocation consists of the identifier xyz in a context compatible with the mode **void**. The trivial but valid program

(**int** x, y, z;
  proc xyz = **void** : $(x := 1; y := 2; z := 3)$;
  xyz; xyz; xyz)

contains three invocations of xyz and is equivalent to

(**int** x, y, z;
  $(x := 1; y := 2; z := 3)$;
  $(x := 1; y := 2; z := 3)$;
  $(x := 1; y := 2; z := 3)$)

At each invocation, xyz (mode **proc void**) is in effect converted to a **void** value; it is thus said to undergo the coercion of DEPROCEDURING.

Global identifiers which appear in a routine text, as in xyz, do not have to be declared at a textually earlier point in the program. It is necessary only that their declarations appear in the same or an enclosing range and that they will have been elaborated by the time the procedure is invoked.

The procedure declared by

proc $sum3in$ = **int** : (**int** x, y, z; $read((x, y, z))$); $x + y + z$)

has the mode **proc int** and uses three variables which are local to the unit in the routine text. It can be invoked by writing the identifier $sum3in$ in a context suitable for an integer value. Thus the phrase

int i = $sum3in$

involves deproceduring $sum3in$ from **proc int** to **int** and is equivalent to

int i = (**int** x,y,z; $read((x,y,z))$); $x + y + z$)

In the case of

real $x := $ *sum3in*

the value obtained by deproceduring is widened, and in

skip; *sum3in*; **skip**

it is voided. An invocation of *sum3in* can thus be either an expression or a statement, whereas an invocation of *xyz* can only be a statement.

Routines may deliver values of any mode. The procedure declared by

proc *readmn* = [,]**int** : ([*m*,*n*] **int** *mult*; *read* (*mult*); *mult*)

has the mode **proc** [,]**int** and delivers a two-dimensional integer multiple. Note that no bounds are specified by the declarer at the beginning of the routine text. The identifiers *m* and *n* are global, while *mult* is local to the routine. The procedure is invoked in the slice

readmn[*1,1*]

where the subscripting operations follow the deproceduring of *readmn* to [,]**int**; the yielded value is the first value input by the routine.

The following procedure delivers the name represented by a global variable:

proc *a or b* = **ref int** : **if** $a < b$ **then** *a* **else** *b* **fi**

Either *a* or *b* (assumed to be of mode **ref int**) is delivered, depending on which one refers to the smaller value at the time of the invocation. Thus

a or b := *20*

is equivalent to

$(a < b \mid a \mid b) := 20$

and

int $c := a$ *or* b

is equivalent to

int $c := (a < b \mid a \mid b)$

In the latter case, the delivered name is dereferenced.

A routine cannot deliver a name which is local to it; for example,

proc *wrong* = **ref int** : (**int** *i*; *read* (*i*); *i*)

is illegal because the name represented by *i* exists only during the elaboration of the unit in the routine text. This problem can be overcome by replacing the declarer **int** with **heap int**:

proc *right* = **ref int** : (**heap int** *i*; *read* (*i*); *i*)

The symbol **heap** may appear at the beginning of any variable declaration. The generated name does not then cease to exist upon completion of the local range; it is in fact a 'globally generated' name which can be used by any part of the program. It is still the case, however, that the identifier *i* is local to the routine; i.e., the global name is represented by the variable *i* only within the routine text. The delivered name will therefore become inaccessible after the elaboration of

print (*right* **plusab** 5)

whereas the identity declaration

ref int *j* = *right*

will associate it with a different variable *j* outside the routine. More will be said about globally generated names in 6.2.2.

Exercises

1. Declare procedures which deliver
   (a) the sum of two global values yielded by *x* and *y*
   (b) the sum of two input values.
2. Write a procedure which inputs and outputs ten numbers. Include it in a program which does nothing but invoke it three times.
3. (a) Write a procedure which generates and delivers the name of a one-dimensional integer multiple of *n* elements, where the value of *n* and the elements are obtained from the input data.
   (b) Write an identity declaration for a multiple variable *v* which invokes this procedure.

5.2.2 Procedures With Parameters

The actions carried out by a procedure may depend on values passed to it

as PARAMETERS. The declarer in the routine text of a procedure with parameters is preceded by a parenthesized list of one or more items separated by
commas, where each item consists of a declarer followed by an identifier.
The identifier is called a FORMAL PARAMETER, and the declarer specifies
its mode. The procedure declared by

> **proc** *pr* = (**int** *a*, **real** *b*) **void**:
> *print* $((a + b, a - b, a * b))$

has an integer formal parameter *a* and a real formal parameter *b* and delivers
no value. The mode of *pr* is written as **proc(int,real)void**, and the equivalent
longer declaration is

> **proc(int,real)void** *pr* = (**int** *a*, **real** *b*) **void**:
> *print* $((a + b, a - b, a * b))$

A unit which invokes a procedure with parameters is termed a CALL
of the procedure and in the simplest case consists of the procedure identifier
followed by a parenthesized list of ACTUAL PARAMETERS separated by
commas. An actual parameter may be any unit yielding (after any necessary
coercions) a value of the mode of the corresponding formal parameter. The
number of actual parameters must be the same as the number of formal
parameters. The call

> *pr* $(i := 10, 5)$

is equivalent to

> (**int** *a* = $i := 10$, **real** *b* = 5;
> *print* $((a + b, a - b, a * b))$)

It can be seen that the unit specified in the routine text is effectively preceded
by a list of identity declarations, each with a formal parameter on the left
side and the corresponding actual parameter on the right side. Note that
in this case *i* will be dereferenced and 5 widened. Note also that the formal
parameters act as local constants and are therefore independent of any
other identifiers *a* and *b* in the program. The effect of the call is to print the
values *15.0*, *5.0* and *50.0* in floating point form.

As a second example, the following procedure, of mode **proc(int)void**,
inputs and immediately outputs a number of values specified by the actual
parameter:

> **proc** *copy* = (**int** *n*) **void**: (

```
    int x;
    to n do read (x); print (x) od )
```

The call *copy(50)* is then equivalent to

```
( int n  =  50; (
  int x;
  to n do read (x); print (x) od ) )
```

Since *n* is a constant in the above example, it would not be possible to change its value within the routine. To enable the value of an actual parameter which is a variable to be changed as a result of elaborating a call, the corresponding formal parameter should be specified as having a reference mode. Here is a declaration of a procedure, with mode **proc(int, int,ref int,ref int) void**, which computes the quotient and corresponding remainder of a pair of integers:

```
    proc divide  =  (int a, int b, ref int q, ref int r) void:
      (q := a ÷ b; r := a mod b)
```

The call

```
    divide (i, j, quot, rem)
```

where all the parameters are integer variables, is equivalent to

```
    (int a  =  i, int b  =  j, ref int q  =  quot, ref int r  =  rem;
      (q := a ÷ b; r := a mod b) )
```

It thus has the same effect as

```
    quot := i ÷ j; rem := i mod j
```

Note that the statement

```
    divide (i, j, 5, rem)
```

is illegal because it implicitly requires the elaboration of the invalid identity declaration

```
    ref int q  =  5
```

When two or more successive formal parameters in a routine text are specified as having the same mode, an abbreviated notation similar to that for declarations may be used. Thus *divide* is more concisely declared by

proc *divide* = (**int** *a*, *b*, **ref int** *q*, *r*) **void** :
    (*q* := *a* ÷ *b*; *r* := *a* **mod** *b*)

The following procedure delivers the smallest of three numbers to be supplied as actual parameters:

proc *min* = (**int** *a*, *b*, *c*) **int** :
    if *a* < *b*
    then if *b* < *c* **then** *a*
        elif *a* < *c* **then** *a* **else** *c* **fi**
    elif *a* < *c* **then** *b*
    elif *b* < *c* **then** *b* **else** *c*
    fi

The mode of *min* is **proc(int,int,int)int**. The statement

i := *1* + *min* (*j*, *k*, *100*)

contains a call of *min* and is thus equivalent to

i := *1* + (**int** *a* = *j*, *b* = *k*, *c* = *100*;
            (*a* < *b* | (*b* < *c* | *a* |: *a* < *c* | *a* | *c*)
            |: *a* < *c* | *b* |: *b* < *c* | *b* | *c*))

When a formal parameter has a row mode, a call of the procedure will cause it to form the left side of an implicit identity declaration involving multiples. Thus no bounds are included in the declarer. The following procedure, of mode **proc([ ]int)int**, delivers the sum of the elements of any one-dimensional integer multiple:

proc *add1* = ([ ] **int** *a*) **int** : (
    int *s* := *0*;
    for *i* **from lwb** *a* **to upb** *a* **do** *s* **plusab** *a*[*i*] **od** ;
    s)

The call

add1 ((*1*, *2*, *4*, *8*))

where the actual parameter is a row display, involves the implicit identity declaration

[ ] **int** *a* = (*1, 2, 4, 8*)

and yields *15*. As the example illustrates, the operators **lwb** and **upb** are often useful in routine texts for determining bounds of multiple parameters.

In some implementations, the above procedure is not as efficient as it could be, because the implicit identity declaration involves the creation of a new copy of the multiple supplied as the actual parameter. In this and many other cases, it would then be better to use a reference to a multiple rather than the multiple itself as a parameter, even when it is not altered within the routine:

```
proc add2 = (ref [] int a) int : (
    int s := 0;
    for i from lwb a to upb a do s plusab a[i] od;
    s )
```

Now

add2 ((*1, 2, 4, 8*))

is not a valid call, but it might be replaced by

[*4*] **int** *b* := (*1, 2, 4, 8*);
add2 (*b*)

The implicit identity declaration is

ref [ ] **int** *a* = *b*

which simply identifies the variables *a* and *b* and does not create a new copy of the elements of *b*.

In the last procedure, it is not possible for the value of an actual parameter to be a flexible name. If the actual name is expected to be flexible, this must be indicated in the mode of the formal parameter:

ref flex [ ] **int** *a*

The following procedure, of mode **proc(ref flex [,] int)void**, transposes (i.e., interchanges the rows and columns) of a flexible table of integers:

```
proc transpose = (ref flex [,] int t ¢ with any lower bounds ¢) void : (
    int m = 1 upb t[at 1], n = 2 upb t[at 1];
    [n,m] int t1;
```

for i **to** n **do** $t1[i,] := t[\textbf{at } 1, \textbf{ at } 1]\,[,i]$ **od**;
$t := t1 \; \cent$ with lower bounds of $1 \; \cent$)

Exercises

1. Given the declaration

   proc $p = (\textbf{int } a, b, c, \textbf{ ref int } d)$ **void**:
       $d := (a \mid a + b, a - b, a * b \mid 0)$

   write units which are equivalent to each of the following calls:
   (a) $p\,(w, x, y, z)$
   (b) $p\,(i := j, e$ **plusab** $f, 5, k)$
2. Declare a procedure *arith* which has two integer parameters a and b and assigns the values of $a+b, a-b, a*b$, and $a \div b$ to four other parameters. Give an example of a call of this procedure.
3. Write a procedure which delivers the multiple obtained by subtracting an integer b from each element of a one-dimensional multiple a.
4. Write a procedure which, given two integer multiples a and b of the same size and lower bounds of 1, delivers a Boolean multiple c, where the value of $c[i]$ is **true** if $a[i] > b[i]$ and **false** otherwise.

5.2.3 Other Aspects of Procedures

Procedure modes have the same status as other modes. Thus, although no example will be given here, it would be possible to declare a multiple of routines given perhaps by a row display of routine texts. In an invocation of one of the procedures, a slice of the procedure multiple would be followed by the actual parameters if any.

Procedures which take routines as parameters or deliver them as values are sometimes useful. The one declared below will tabulate a given integer function f for arguments ranging between two given integers i and j:

    proc $tab = (\textbf{proc(int)int } f, \textbf{ int } i, j)$ **void** :
      for k **from** i **to** j **do** $print\,((k, f(k), newline))$ **od**

The first actual parameter in a call of *tab* could be the identifier of any procedure of mode **proc(int)int**. It could also be a routine text, as in the call

    $tab\,((\textbf{int } x) \textbf{ int } : 2 * x, -5, 5)$

A procedure may call itself or some other procedure which when called results in another invocation of the first procedure. This phenomenon is called RECURSION. A simple example is provided by the following procedure which computes the factorial function:

proc *fact* = (**int** *n*) **int**:
$(n = 0 \mid 1 \mid n * fact (n - 1))$

The call *fact*(2) will result in the elaboration of *fact*(1) before the completion of the first invocation, and this in turn will result in the elaboration of *fact*(0). This third-level invocation will deliver the value *1*, so that the second-level invocation will deliver *1*, so that the original call will yield *2*. There is no confusion of parameter values at the different levels: only the one at the current level is accessible. The same would be true for any other identifier local to the procedure. Practical uses of recursion are somewhat specialized, but it enables some procedures to be programmed very concisely.

The identifiers of all the procedures considered so far have been constants. It is also possible to declare a procedure variable:

proc(int)int *vp*

The mode of *vp* is **ref proc(int)int**. The variable declaration may of course specify an initial routine value, given by an appropriate previously declared procedure identifier or by a routine text. In the latter case, the initializing declaration may be written in the following alternative form:

proc identifier := routine-text

Thus we may write

proc *vp* := (**int** *n*) **int**: (**int** *i, j* := 0;
    to *n* **do** *read* (*i*); *j* **plusab** *i* **od**; *j*)

In a call such as *vp*(5), *vp* will first be dereferenced. The name can later be assigned another routine of mode **proc(int)int**,

$vp := (\textbf{int } a) \textbf{ int} : (a + 1) \div 2$

so that a call *vp*(5) will then invoke a completely different procedure. The right side of the above assignment could also be the identifier of a **proc(int)int** declared previously, and if the mode of *vp2* is also **ref proc(int)int**, the statement

$vp := vp2$

involves dereferencing *vp2*. (Note that for procedures without parameters, such an assignment would not involve any deproceduring.) Since routines cannot be transput and there are no predefined operators for them, constant procedures are adequate for most purposes.

The scope rules for procedure identifiers are the same as for other identifiers, and a procedure can be invoked at a given point in a program only if it is accessible at that point. However, a subtle type of error can arise when certain assignments to procedure names are attempted in inner ranges:

proc(int)void p;
(int $i := 5$; $p := $ **(int** j) **void** : $print$ $(j * i))$;
p (10)

Even though the call is within the scope of the variable p, it cannot succeed because the routine must access a name i which no longer exists. The assignation with p on the left side is in fact illegal in this case. Such problems cannot arise if only constant procedures are declared.

Exercises

1. (a) Declare a procedure p which delivers the routine represented by

   (int a, b) **int** : $a * a + b * b$

   if the value of p's parameter is **true**, and

   (int a, b) **int** : $a * a - b * b$

   otherwise.
   (b) Write an expression containing a call of p which is a call of the delivered routine.
2. The number of combinations of n things taken r at a time is equal to n if $r = 1$, and $(n-r+1) \div r$ multiplied by the number of combinations of n things taken $r-1$ at a time otherwise. Write a recursive procedure to compute this function.

5.3 Operators

Routines can be associated with operator symbols as well as with procedure identifiers. Operators are represented by indicants such as **abs** and **plusab** or by special symbols such as $+$ and $< =$. We have encountered many predefined operators, each of which corresponds to a routine to carry out some computation on its operands and deliver a result. This section

explains how the programmer can define his own operators by means of
OPERATION DECLARATIONS.

Every dyadic operator corresponds to a routine with two formal parameters, and every monadic operator corresponds to a routine with one
formal parameter. When an operator is used in a formula, its operand or
operands are analogous to the actual parameters in a procedure call. Operator routines usually deliver values, but this is not strictly required. An
operation declaration is similar to an identity declaration for a procedure
except that the symbol **op** is used in place of **proc**. For example,

```
op max  =  ([ ]int a) int  : (
   int m := a[lwb a];
   for i from lwb a + 1 to upb a do
      if a[i] > m then m := a[i] fi od;
   m )
```

defines a monadic operator **max** which will deliver the largest element of a
one-dimensional integer multiple with at least one element. Now the formula

$$\text{max } ([\,]\text{ int } a = (-5, 10, 50, 7, 0); a)$$

will yield *50*.

In contrast to procedure identifiers, an operator symbol may be associated
with more than one routine at the same time, and most of the predefined
symbols have this property. Each associated routine must have a different
mode; for example, = represents routines with the modes **proc(int,int)bool**,
proc(real,real)bool, **proc(real,int)bool**, and so on. A given symbol may
represent both monadic and dyadic operators, except that $<, >, =, *,$
and $\times$ cannot be monadic symbols (or the first character thereof). When
a symbol represents several dyadic operators, the priority is the same for
all of them. Thus the following additional version of = will also have priority *4*:

```
op  =  =  ([ ] int a, b) bool :
   if int m = upb a[at 1], n = upb b[at 1]; m = n
   then bool f := true;
      for i to m while f do
         if a[at 1] [i] ≠ b[at 1] [i]
         then f := false fi
      od;
      f
   else false
   fi
```

The priority of a new dyadic operator symbol must be specified by a PRIORITY DECLARATION of the form

  prio symbol $=$ digit

where the digit is between *1* and *9*. As an example, we may declare a priority and two routines for the symbol **max**:

  prio max $=9$;
  op max $=$ (**int** a, b) **int** : $(a > b \mid a \mid b)$;
  op max $=$ (**real** a, b) **real** : $(a > b \mid a \mid b)$

A priority declaration can also be used to redefine the priority of existing dyadic operators. A sequence of two or more operation declarations can be combined, with **op** appearing only once, so that the last two lines above could be replaced by

  op max $=$ (**int** a, b) **int** : $(a > b \mid a \mid b)$,
    max $=$ (**real** a, b) **real** : $(a > b \mid a \mid b)$

When an operator symbol associated with several routines is used in a formula, the routine which is actually invoked depends on the modes of the operands. Thus *5* **max** *6* is equivalent to

  (**int** $a = 5, b = 6; (a > b \mid a \mid b))$

and yields *6*, while *2.4 max 9.0* is equivalent to

  (**real** $a = 2.4, b = 9.0; (a > b \mid a \mid b))$

and yields *9.0*. The coercions of dereferencing and deproceduring (as well as uniting, which is introduced in the next chapter) may be applied to make the modes of the operands match those required by one of the routines. Thus if *i* is an integer variable, *i* **max** *5* is a valid formula invoking the **proc** (**int**,**int**)**int** version of **max**. Widening and rowing are not applicable to operands. Thus *2.4* **max** *i* is erroneous since **max** does not have a routine permitting a real left operand and an integer right operand. We could of course declare such an operator. It should also be recalled that the phenomenon of balancing described in 4.3.1 is applicable when an operand is a conditional clause or case clause.

An operator symbol cannot simultaneously represent two routines where the modes of the formal parameters would permit the construction of ambiguous formulas. For example, we cannot declare the additional operator

```
op max  =  (ref int a, int b) int :
    a := (a > b |a| b)
```

in the same range as the previous ones because then the formula *i* **max** 5 would be consistent with both the **proc(int,int)int** version and the **proc(ref int,int)int** version of **max**. If both these operators are wanted, different symbols must be used for them.

The scope of an operator symbol, like that of an identifier, is limited to the range in which it is declared. A declaration for a given symbol in an inner range renders inaccessible any existing operators with the same or related (e.g., **int** and **ref int**) operand modes.

Exercises

1. Define an operator which delivers the sum of the values referred to by two given integer names.
2. Declare addition operators for pairs of any combination of integer and real multiples with ten elements.

5.4 Non-numeric Examples (SCO)

The predefined procedures *whole*, *fixed*, and *float*, which were first encountered in 2.2.2, all deliver string values. The additional predefined procedure *char in string*, of mode **proc(char,ref int,string)bool**, tests whether a given character occurs in a given string; if so, it assigns the subscript of the leftmost occurrence to the second parameter and delivers **true**. As a generalization of *char in string*, *index* as declared below tests whether one string *s1* occurs as a substring of a second string *s2*:

```
proc index  =  (string s1, ref int i, string s2)bool : (
    int m  =  upb s1[at 1] − 1;
    bool not found := true;
    for k from lwb s2 to upb s2  −  m while not found do
      if s1  =  s2[k:k+m]
      then i := k; not found := false
      fi
    od;
    not not found )
```

The operator declared as follows will remove all trailing blanks from a given string:

```
op trim  =  (string s) string : (
```

```
int i := upb s;
from upb s by − 1 to lwb s
  while s[i] = blank
  do i minusab 1 od;
s[:i] )
```

The next operator converts a string assumed to consist entirely of digit characters to the corresponding integer value:

```
op num = (string s) int : (
  ¢ assume abs yields consecutive values for digits ¢
  int zero = abs "0"; int val := 0;
  for i from lwb s to upb s do
    val := val * 10 + abs s[i] − zero od;
  val )
```

The following procedure sorts a multiple of strings into alphabetical order using the 'bubble' method described in 4.4.1 for the case of integer data:

```
proc alphsort = (ref [ ] string rs) void : (
  bool active := true; string temp;
  for j from upb rs − 1 by −1 to 1 while active do
    active := false;
    for i to j do
      ref string rsi = rs[i], rsi1 = rs[i + 1);
      if rsi > rsi1
      then temp := rsi;
        rsi := rsi1;
        rsi1 := temp;
        active := true
      fi
    od
  od )
```

Exercises

1. Define an operator to remove all leading blanks from a given string.
2. Using *char in string*, write a sequence of phrases which, given a string *s* with no leading or trailing blanks, prints each segment of *s* containing no blanks on a separate line.
3. Write a procedure to append a string to the multiple of strings, with lower bound *1*, referred to by a flexible name.

4. In a 'binary search' for a given value in a sorted set of values, the middle element is tested first; if it is not the desired value, then the middle element of either the first or the second half of the set is tested, depending on the result of the first test. This process continues until either the desired value is found or the subset of elements being searched shrinks to nothing. Write a procedure to search a multiple of strings with lower bound *1* for a given string, delivering the position number of the string if it is in the set and *0* otherwise.

5.5 Numeric Examples (NUM)

As simple examples of operation declarations, we may define exponentiation to a real power:

op ↑ = (**real** *a*, *b*) **real** : *exp* (*b* * *ln* (*a*)),
   ↑ = (**int** *a*, **real** *b*) **real** : *exp* (*b* * *ln* (*a*))

The operation is meaningful only when the left operand is positive; if it is not, an error will occur within the procedure *ln*.

The predefined procedures such as *ln* which were introduced in 2.3.5 all have the mode **proc(real)real**. There is an additional procedure *random*, of mode **proc real**, which delivers some number less than *1* and greater than or equal to *0*. When *random* is invoked a large number of times, the delivered values will tend to be uniformly distributed over this interval. This is useful in a broad class of simulation problems. As a simple example, the following program simulates 5000 throws of a set of three dice and prints the percentage of throws resulting in each possible total:

```
(proc throw = int : entier (1 + random * 6);
[3:18] int totals;
totals [at 1] := (0, 0, 0, 0, 0, 0, 0, 0, 0, 0, 0, 0, 0, 0, 0, 0);
to 5000 do totals [throw + throw + throw] plusab 1 od;
for i from 3 to 18 do
  print ((newline, whole(i, −2), ":",
    fixed(totals[i]/50,−8, 1), "%"))
od )
```

The random numbers are actually generated by the predefined procedure *next random*, of mode **proc(ref int)real**, which changes the value of its parameter to some new value between *0* and *max int* and delivers the result of mapping that value into a real number between *0* and *1*. The procedure *random* is defined as

proc *random* = **real** : *next random* (*last random*) where *last random* is an environment enquiry of mode **ref int** with the initial value

  round (*max int* / 2)

Procedures with routines as parameter values are often useful in numerical work. As an example, suppose we require a simple procedure which will numerically integrate any well-behaved real function *f* over any interval (*a,b*) using the 'trapezoidal' rule

$$\text{area} = h \left(\frac{f(a) + f(b)}{2} + f(a + h) + f(a + 2h) + \ldots + f(a + (n - 1)h) \right)$$

where the accuracy of the result increases with *n*, and

$$h = (b - a) / n$$

The procedure may be written as follows:

  proc *trap* = (**proc(real)real** *f*, **real** *a*, *b*, **int** *n*) **real** : (
  real *h* = (*b* − *a*) / *n*;
  real *x* := *a*, *s* := (*f*(*a*) + *f*(*b*)) / 2;
  to *n* − *1* **do** *x* **plusab** *h*; *s* **plusab** *f*(*x*) **od**;
  h ∗ *s*)

The following sequence shows how *trap* might be used to integrate e^{-x^2} between *0* and *0.7*:

  proc *func* = (**real** *x*) **real** : *exp* (−*x* ∗ *x*);
  real *result* = *trap* (*func*, 0, 0.7, 200)

If *func* is not used for any other purpose, it is just as well to use the routine text in the call:

  real *result* = *trap* ((**real** *x*) **real** : *exp* (−*x* ∗ *x*), 0,0.7, 200)

Now consider the use of operators for the manipulation of matrices. If, for example, *x*, *y*, and *z* are three matrices with the same bounds, it is more convenient to write a formula such as *x* + *y* + *z* than a nested call such as *add*(*add*(*x*,*y*),*z*). Assuming that efficiency considerations dictate that the formal parameters of such an operator have reference modes, the delivered value should be the name of the result matrix rather than the result itself; otherwise, a formula such as $x + y + z$ with more than one matrix operator symbol would not be valid. The delivered name must be generated globally within the routine. In the following declaration of an operator for matrix multiplication, the bounds of the parameters are checked for compatibility and the lower bounds are required to be *1*:

```
op ∗ = (ref [,] real a, b) ref [,] real :
  if int m = 1 upb a, n = 2 upb a, p = 2 upb b;
    1 lwb a = 1 and 2 lwb a = 1 and 1 lwb b = 1
    and 2 lwb b = 1 and 1 upb b = n
  then heap [m,p] real c;
    for i to m do
      ref [ ] real arow = a[i,];
      for j to p do
        ref [ ] real bcol = b[,j];
        ref real cij = c[i, j] := 0;
        for k to n do cij plusab arow[k] ∗ bcol [k] od
      od
    od;
    c
  fi
```

Exercises

1. Declare an operator to find the mean of the elements of a one-dimensional real multiple.
2. In the Newton–Raphson interative method for finding a zero x of a real function f, each new approximation is obtained by evaluating

   $$x - f(x) / g(x),$$

   where g is the derivative function of f. Assuming that procedures for f and g have already been declared, write a general procedure for this method.
3. Declare an addition operator for pairs of triangular matrices (see 3.3.8).

Chapter 6

Extended Modes

6.1 Mode Declarations

There are several methods by which new modes can be defined in terms of old ones. Some modes, such as **int**, **real**, and **bool**, are 'primitive' or unanalyzable, while others, such as the procedure modes and the row modes, are built up from these with the aid of auxiliary symbols such as **proc**, [, and]. In this chapter, the remaining methods for forming new modes and some of the uses of such modes are described.

It is often convenient to invent completely new indicants for complicated modes. This is done by means of MODE DECLARATIONS of the form

    mode indicant = declarer

where the declarer specifies the mode to be represented by the new indicant. For example, the mode declaration

    mode intfn = **proc(int)int**

defines **intfn** as an alternative representation of the mode **proc(int)int** within the current range. The new symbol can be used in the same ways as any other mode symbol in that range. For example, the identity declaration

    proc p = (**intfn** a) **int** : $a(a(a(5)))$

is equivalent to

    proc p = (**proc(int)int** a) **int** : $a(a(a(5)))$

When the declarer in a mode declaration specifies a row mode, it must contain expressions for bounds:

    mode table = $[m,n]$ **int**

The bounds are elaborated only when the new symbol is later used. Thus if the values of *m* and *n* are *10* and *20* when the variable declaration **table** *a* is elaborated, this phrase is equivalent to

[*10, 20*] **int** *a*

The indicant **table** may also be used in contexts where bounds are not to be included, as in

table *b* = *a*

In this case, the bounds in the mode declaration are ignored, and the effect is the same as

[,] **int** *b* = *a*

A part of a declarer beginning with the symbol **ref** never contains bounds. Thus we could have

mode tablename = **ref** [,] **int**

The right side of a mode declaration may begin with the symbol **flex**:

mode bunch = **flex** [*1:0*] **int**

If the indicant is later used in a context where the declarer would not be valid, the **flex** will be ignored. Thus

bunch *c* = (*1, 2, 3, 4, 5*)

is equivalent to

[ ] **int** = (*1, 2, 3, 4, 5*)

On the other hand,

ref bunch *d* = *e* := (*1, 2, 3, 4, 5*)

is equivalent to

ref flex [ ] **int** *d* = *e* := (*1, 2, 3, 4, 5*)

The indicant **string** is predefined as

> **mode string = flex** [*1:0*] **char**

Circular sequences of mode declarations such as

> **mode abc = def**;
> **mode def = abc**

as well as something like

> **mode abc = ref abc**

are not allowed and would not be of any use anyway. Meaningful sequences such as

> **mode m1 =** [*10*] **int**;
> **mode m2 = flex** [*1:0*] **int**;
> **mode m3 =** [*n*] **int**

may be combined into one phrase:

> **mode m1 =** [*10*] **int**,
> **m2 = flex** [*1:0*] **int**,
> **m3 =** [*n*] **int**

6.2 Manipulation of Names

6.2.1 Pointers and Casts

A new mode can be derived by prefacing any other mode with the symbol **ref**. All the simple reference modes such as

> **ref int**
> **ref** [,] **bool**
> **ref proc**(**int**)**void**

are obtained in this way. Names may themselves be referred to by other names, which must then have modes such as

> **ref ref int**

ref ref [,] bool
ref ref proc(int)void

It is convenient to use the term POINTER for names or variables which are or which represent names of names, i.e., objects whose modes begin with two or more **ref**s.

The variable declaration

ref int $p1, p2$

defines $p1$ and $p2$ as pointers which can refer to any integer names as values. If the mode of i is **ref int**, it can be assigned to $p1$ without being dereferenced:

$p1 := i$

In every assignation, the right side must yield a value whose mode begins with one less **ref** than the mode yielded by the left side. All coercions are permitted for the value on the right, but only deproceduring is allowed on the left. Thus $p1 := 5$ is invalid, but if the intention is to assign 5 to the current value of $p1$ (i.e., the name i), this can be done by replacing $p1$ with a construct called a CAST to force dereferencing to the required mode:

ref int $(p1) := 5$

A cast is a unit of the form

declarer enclosed-clause

where an ENCLOSED CLAUSE is either a closed clause, conditional clause, case clause, or loop clause (or a conformity clause, to be introduced in 6.4, or a collateral clause or parallel clause, to be introduced in 8.3). The value of a cast is the value of its enclosed clause, and all coercions are permitted in order that the mode will be that specified by the declarer. A cast can be used to force coercions in any context where they could not otherwise occur. For example, if **mon** is a monadic operator defined only for real operands and i is an integer variable, then the cast in the formula

mon real (i)

permits widening to take place after dereferencing. The use of a cast also allows the value of an operand to be that yielded by a row display:

upb [ ]**int** $(i, j, 5)$

Returning now to pointers, in the assignation $p2 := p1$, $p1$ is dereferenced to yield the name i, which is assigned to $p2$. Both pointers now indirectly refer to 5 through their common value i. In $i := p1$ or $i := p1 + 5$, $p1$ must be dereferenced twice in succession to yield a value of the required mode **int**.

When a name is assigned to a pointer, the scope of the former must be at least as large as the scope of the latter. If this were not so, a scope problem similar to that described in 5.2.3 for procedure variables could arise.

Values which are names cannot be transput. In the statement $print(p1)$, $p1$ will be dereferenced twice and the resulting integer printed. In $read(p1)$, it will be dereferenced once and an integer value for the resulting name will be input.

The following variable declaration defines a pointer (mode **ref ref** [ ] **int**) to a multiple value:

ref [ ] **int** pm

Note that no bounds are given after a **ref** symbol; pm may refer to any non-flexible name of a one-dimensional integer multiple. Suppose now that we have

[5] **int** $a := (2, 4, 8, 16, 32)$;
$pm := a$

If pm is trimmed or subscripted, it will first be dereferenced once; for example, $pm[4]$ is equivalent to

ref [ ] **int** (pm) [4]

or $a[4]$, and all of these slices yield 16. In the assignation $pm := i$, the integer name i will be rowed from **ref int** to **ref** [ ] **int**, where the bounds are [1:1].

The pointer pm could also refer to the name of a submultiple:

$pm := a[3:]$

In such cases, the trimmed multiple variable must not be flexible.

To illustrate further the generality of the reference modes, we may declare a variable referring to a multiple of integer names:

[3] **ref int** $mn := (i, j, k)$

We could equally well generate a name of a multiple of names of integer multiples, as in

[*n*] **ref** [ ] **int** *mnm*

or even a name of a multiple of pointers:

[*n*] **ref ref int** *mpn*

Exercises

1. Write declarations for new mode symbols for pointers to integers, real numbers, Boolean values, and integer names.
2. If *i* is a **ref int**, *ip* a **ref ref int**, and *a* a **ref** [ ] **int**, identify the coercions involved in each of the following:
   (a) *ip* := *i* :=5
   (b) **ref int** (*ip*) := *i* := 5
   (c) *a*[*ip*] := *i*
   (d) *ip* := *a*[5]

3. If the identifiers are as above, point out the errors in each of the following:
   (a) *ip* := 5
   (b) **int** (*ip*) := 5
   (c) **ref real** (*ip*) := 5.0

6.2.2 Generators

We have already seen that names can be created by means of variable declarations such as **int** *x* and **heap int** *x*. A name created in this way always has a variable (identifier) associated with it, at least within the range of the declaration (see 5.2.1). We have also seen that a name may correspond to more than one variable if an identity declaration such as

ref int *y* = *x*

is in effect. On the other hand, it is possible for a name never to correspond to any identifier at all; such a name may be created by a LOCAL GENERTAOR, which is an expression consisting of the symbol **loc** followed by a declarer (which includes bounds wherever possible). The value yielded by a generator is the name it creates, and this name ceases to exist upon completion of the smallest surrounding range which contains a declaration. As an example, **loc int** is a local generator yielding a name of mode **ref int**. The name can be assigned to a pointer, as in

p2 := **loc int**

and an integer value can be assigned to the name:

ref int (*p2*) := *15*

These two assignments (in reverse order) can also be specified in one unit:

p2 := **loc int** := *15*

A GLOBAL GENERATOR contains the symbol **heap** in place of **loc**; thus the expression **heap int** is a global generator. Like a local generator, a global generator creates a new name and yields it as its value, but the name does not disappear upon completion of the smallest surrounding range containing a declaration. After the elaboration of the statements

p2 := **heap int**; *p2* := *p3*

the generated name will continue to exist for an indefinite time but be completely inaccessible. If a program globally generates so many names that the storage available for that purpose becomes exhausted, all the inaccessible names will automatically be cleared away by a process known as 'garbage collection'. This may well result in decreased efficiency for programs which contain global generators.

A variable declaration can begin with a generator rather than a declarer. Examples involving global generators have already been given in the last chapter. In the case of local generators, the effect is the same as when the symbol **loc** is omitted.

It is clearly possible to write identity declarations such as

ref int *j* = **loc int**

and a little thought will confirm that this has exactly the same effect as **loc int** *j* or **int** *j*. Every variable declaration is in fact equivalent to an identity declaration with a generator on the right side and a declarer for the full mode of the variable, beginning with at least one **ref**, preceding the identifier on the left side. The following list contains a variety of pairs of equivalent declarations:

bool *x*	**ref bool** *x* = **loc bool**
int *x, y*	**ref int** *x* = **loc int**, **ref int** *y* = **loc int**
real *x* := *0*	**ref real** *x* = **loc real** := *0*
ref int *x*	**ref ref int** *x* = **loc ref int**
[*n*] **int** *x*	**ref** [ ] **int** *x* = **loc** [*n*] **int**

flex [*1*:*0*] **bool** *x*   **ref flex** [ ] **bool** *x* = **loc flex** [*1*:*0*] **bool**
ref [ ] **int** *pm*   **ref ref** [ ] **int** *pm* = **loc ref** [ ] **int**

There are analogous equivalent forms for the global generation of names; for example,

heap int *j*

is equivalent to

ref int *j* = **heap int**

Note that the generated name will be inaccessible after the completion of the unit

(**heap int** *j*; *read* (*j*))

However, it will continue to be accessible if it is assigned to a global pointer *p1*:

(**heap int** *j*; *read* (*j*); *p1* := *j*)

Assuming that this unit is to be used as a statement, the same effect is achieved by

read (*p1* := **heap int**)

6.2.3 Identity Relations (SCO)

To test the value of a pointer, we must have some means of comparing names. The operators = and ≠ will not do because their operands are always completely dereferenced; for example, in *p1* = *i*, *p1* (mode **ref ref int**) will be dereferenced twice and *i* (mode **ref int**) once, and the formula would yield **true** if *p1* referred to some other name *j* which happened to have the same value as *i*. The desired comparison is carried out by an IDENTITY RELATION, which consists of a pair of expressions yielding names separated by the symbol **is** (which may also be written as : = :) or by **isnt** (also written as : ≠ : or :/ = :). An identity relation is a unit yielding a Boolean value; if *p1* refers to *i*, then *p1* **is** *i* yields **true** and *i* **isnt** *p1* yields **false**.

The symbols **is** and **isnt** are not operators, and identity relations, like assignations, must be parenthesized when they are used as operands:

(*p 1* **is** *i*) **and** (*p 2* **is** *j*)

Pairs of names (but only names) of any mode can be compared by means of these constructs. If, as above, the modes on the two sides are not the same, dereferencing (and all other coercions) is permitted only on one side; only deproceduring is allowed on the other side. (This is similar to the situation for assignations, except that the 'left' side may actually be either the left or the right side of an identity relation.) If both modes are the same, no coercions take place before the comparison. Thus *p1* **is** *p2*, where *p2* is another integer pointer, always yields **false** even if *p1* and *p2* refer to the same name. To compare the current values of *p1* and *p2*, a cast may be used on at least one side of the relation; any of the following units will do:

> **ref int** (*p1*) **is** *p2*
> *p1* **is ref int** (p2)
> **ref int** (*p1*) **is ref int** (*p2*)

There is a special unit, written as **nil** or ○ which represents a name of any required mode but which cannot refer to any value (so that it cannot be assigned to or dereferenced). In the initializing declaration

> **ref int** *p3* := **nil**

nil represents a name of mode **ref int** which refers to no value and is assigned to the pointer *p3*. The symbol **nil** can be used in an identity relation, as in

> **if ref int** (*p3*) **isnt nil**
> **then ref int** (*p3*) := *5*
> **fi**

Note that *p3* **isnt nil** would not have the desired effect since **nil** would then have the mode **ref ref int** and *p3* would not be dereferenced.

6.3 Structured Values

6.3.1 The Definition and Use of Structures

A STRUCTURED VALUE, or STRUCTURE for short, is a set of values, called the FIELDS of the structure, which may have different modes and which are accessed by expressions called SELECTIONS to be described below. A declarer for a structure mode consists of the symbol **struct** followed by a parenthesized list of one or more field specifications separated by commas. Each field specification consists of a declarer, which must not be that of the structure mode itself, followed by a SELECTOR, which is similar in appearance to an identifier. The following are simple examples of structure modes:

    struct (**int** *field 1*, **real** *field 2*)
    struct (**int** *a*, **real** *b*)
    struct (**int** *a*, **int** *b*, **int** *c*)

The selectors are an integral part of the modes; because they contain different selectors, the first two of the above modes are quite distinct and are not coerceable to each other. No confusion arises if the same selector is used in different modes or if a selector is also used as an identifier in the same range. However, the selectors in a given structure mode must be distinct from each other.

Names of structures are generated like names of any other mode; for example,

    struct (**int** *a*, **real** *b*) *st1*

is equivalent to

    ref struct (**int** *a*, **real** *b*) *st1* =
      loc struct (**int** a, **real** *b*)

It is usually more convenient to first declare a new symbol for the structure mode:

    mode ab = **struct** (**int** *a*, **real** *b*)

If two or more successive fields in a structure declarer have the same mode, they can be combined; thus the following mode declarations are equivalent:

    mode triple = **struct** (**int** *a*, **int** *b*, **real** *c*)
    mode triple = **struct** (**int** *a*, *b*, **real** *c*)

The new symbol can be used in declarations of structure variables:

    triple *x*, *y*

The name of a field of a structure can be expressed as a selection of the form

    selector **of** structure-variable

where the selector must be part of the structure's mode. Thus *a* **of** *x* refers to the first field of *x* and has the mode **ref int**, while *c* **of** *y* refers to the third field of *y* and has the mode **ref real**. The field values can be filled in by assignment to these names:

> *a* **of** *x* := *5*;
> *c* **of** *x* := *c* **of** *y* := *4.2*;
> *b* **of** *x* := *a* **of** *x*

Selections can also be used as operands; for example,

> *i* + *a* **of** *x* * *j*

is equivalent to

> *i* + (*a* **of** *x*) * *j*

The construct following the **of** in a selection may be another selection or a slice, with dereferencing and deproceduring being applied if necessary. For example, if *st2* is declared as

> **struct (int** *a*, **ref triple** *b*) *st2*

then

> *a* **of** *b* **of** *st2*

is valid and means the same thing as

> *a* **of ref triple** (*b* **of** *st2*)

Also, if we have the multiple of structures

> [*5*] **triple** *mt*

then *a* **of** *mt*[*3*] is valid. On the other hand, if we have a structure containing a multiple, such as

> **struct (int** *a*, [*5*] **int** *b*) *st3*

then the selection within a slice must be parenthesized:

> (*b* **of** *st3*) [*3*]

A similar situation exists for calls; if we have

> **struct (int** *a*, **proc(int)void** *b*) *st4*

then

(*b* **of** *st4*) (*5*)

is a call of the procedure (as yet undefined) within *st4*, whereas

a **of** *pr* (*5*)

might refer to a field of a structure delivered by a procedure *pr* of mode

proc(int)ref triple.

To assign values simultaneously to an entire structure with at least two fields, we may use a STRUCTURE DISPLAY, which has the same form as a row display:

$x := (15, i + 1, 20)$

Each field of the display may contain any expression which is compatible with the required mode, all coercions being permitted. Since the mode of x is **ref triple** and that of its third field is **real**, *20* will be widened in this case. The statement is in fact equivalent to the three statements

a **of** $x := 15$
b **of** $x := i + 1$
c **of** $x := 20$

elaborated in any order. The statement $y := x$ causes each field of y to be the same value as the corresponding field of x; i.e., it is equivalent to the statements

a **of** $y := a$ **of** x
b **of** $y := b$ **of** x
c **of** $y := c$ **of** x

elaborated in any order.

Structure displays are also useful in initializing and identity declarations. For example,

triple $z = (0, 0, 0)$

defines z as a constant structure. The selections for its fields are also constants; for example, *a* **of** z is an integer constant yielding *0*. It can be seen that the relationship between the modes of structure identifiers and the modes of their selections is analogous to that between the modes of multiple identifiers and the modes of their slices.

It is often useful to define new operators involving structures. The following declaration specifies the field-by-field addition of two triples:

> **op** + = (**triple** p, q) **triple** :
>   (a **of** p + a **of** q,
> b **of** p + b **of** q,
> c **of** p + c **of** q)

Now we may write, for example,

> $x := x + y + z$

A structure display may only appear in contexts where all coercions are permitted, so that it cannot be used as an operand. We therefore have another application for casts:

> z + **triple** (5, 15, 42.7)

Structures provide a useful alternative to multiples when the constituent values have different modes or, even if they all have the same mode, when the position of a value to be accessed can be specified when the program is written (using a selector) as opposed to being computed when the program is elaborated (using a subscript). The amount of data that can be handled using structures is not normally limited by the necessity of providing a selector for each field, for we may employ linked structures (to be described in 6.5), multiples of structures, or structures containing multiples.

In the case of a multiple of structures, a selection containing the multiple variable may be written; it represents the name of a multiple with the elements specified by the selector. For example, if $mt2$ is declared as

> [n] **triple** $mt2$

then the selection

> a **of** $mt2$

has the mode **ref** [ ] **int** with bounds [$1:n$] and elements a **of** $mt2[1]$ through a **of** $mt2[n]$.

A structure variable where the fields have suitable modes (not, for example,

names or routines) may appear in a transput statement. The structure will
be straightened in much the same way as a multiple; for example,

   read ((*i*, *x*, *j*))

where *x* is one of our triples, is equivalent to

   read ((*i*, *a* **of** *x*, *b* **of** *x*, *c* **of** *x*, *j*))

If a field is a multiple or another structure, it will also be straightened before
continuing with the next field.

Exercises

1. Abbreviate each of the following:
   (a) **mode rtl** = **struct** (**int** *num*, **int** *den*)
   (b) **ref struct** (**real** *x*, **int** *y*) *s* =
       loc struct (**real** *x*, **int** *y*)
   (c) **mode bitstr** = **struct** ([*20*] **bool** *b*),
       mode rr = **struct** (**flex** [*1*:*0*] **real** *a*, **int** *b*)
2. Point out the errors in each of the following:
   (a) **mode st** = **struct** (**int** *a*, **st** *b*)
   (b) **mode st** = **struct** (**int** *a*, **real** *a*)
   (c) **ref struct** (**int** *a*, *b*) *x* = **loc struct** (**int** *a*, *c*)
   (d) (*a* **of** *b*) **of** *x*
3. Remove any redundant parentheses from each of the following:
   (a) *a* **of** (*b* **of** *c*)
   (b) *a* **of** (*b*[*i*])
   (c) *a* **of** (*b*(*c*))
   (d) (*a* **of** *b*) (*c*)

6.3.2 Example: Data Processing (SCO)

Structures are often useful in commercial programming because of the
need to manipulate data items containing several values of different modes.
As an example, consider a program which is run once a week or once a
month and computes the payroll of a company with hourly-paid employees.
It is convenient to keep all the relevant information about an employee
in a structure with a mode such as

   mode employee = **struct** (**int** *number*, **string** *name*,
       struct (**string** *line1*, *line2*, *line3*) *address*,
       real *pay rate*, *gross pay to date*,

int *dependants*)

The third field has been specified as having another structure mode so that the three lines of an employee's address, which form a natural group, can be picked out by a single selection. Each structure is assumed to contain all the information necessary (gross pay to date and number of dependants) to calculate the employee's income tax at the same time as his gross pay.

Assuming that all the employee information is held in a multiple of such structures and the corresponding numbers of hours worked during the pay period in an integer multiple of the same size, the following procedure calculates the net pay and updates the accumulated gross pay for all the employees:

```
proc pay = (ref [ ] employee emp, ref [ ] int hours) [ ] real : (
   int n = upb emp; [n] real net pay;
   for i to n do
      ref employee empi = emp[i];
      real gross pay = hours[i] * pay rate of empi;
      gross pay to date of empi plusab gross pay;
      net pay [i] := gross pay − tax (empi, gross pay)
   od;
   net pay )
```

The procedure *tax*, of mode **proc(ref employee, real)real**, must be declared elsewhere. It should be appreciated that a realistic payroll program would be much more complicated than this and would likely make use of some of the advanced transput facilities described in the next chapter.

Exercises

1. Declare a mode suitable for representing information about the books in a library, including author's name, title, publisher, year of publication, date of acquisition, price paid, and decimal classification code.
2. Write a procedure which, given the name of a multiple of items of the above mode, delivers an integer multiple containing all the subscript values corresponding to books which were published in a given year y.

6.3.3. Example: Rational Arithmetic (NUM)

Mathematically, a rational number is an ordered pair of integers sometimes written as p/q. The rational number $5/2$, for example, corresponds to the real number 2.5, $-5/1$ corresponds to -5.0, and $0/b$, where b is any non-zero integer, corresponds to 0.0. In Algol 68, we may define the new mode

mode rtl = **struct** (**int** *num, den*)

and use it as an alternative to **real** in certain applications.

As an example, consider the addition of polynomials with rational coefficients. Given the coefficients of the quadratic polynomials

$$\frac{1}{9}x^2 + \frac{5}{12}x + \frac{1}{7}$$

$$\frac{2}{9}x^2 - \frac{1}{4}x + \frac{2}{7}$$

as data in the form of pairs of integers, the sum is more meaningfully and accurately represented by the rational values

$$1/3 \qquad\qquad 1/6 \qquad\qquad 3/7$$

than by the rounded real values

$$0.3333333 \qquad\qquad 0.1666667 \qquad\qquad 0.4285714$$

For the new mode to be of any use, the various arithmetic operations must be defined for it. Using a structure display, the monadic $-$ is one of the simplest:

op $-$ = (**rtl** *a*) **rtl** : $(-num$ **of** *a, den* **of** *a*)

We adopt the convention that the denominator is always positive, so that the sign of a rational is given by the sign of its numerator.

The product of two rationals p/q and s/t is ps/qt. To prevent the numerators and denominators from becoming too large, the result should be simplified if possible; i.e., both fields should be divided by their greatest common divisor. It so happens that this function is computed by the following recursive procedure:

proc *gcd* = (**int** *a, b*) **int** :
$(b = 0 \mid$ **abs** *a* $\mid$ *gcd* $(b, a$ **mod** $b)$)

Now the multiplication operator can be declared as

op * = (**rtl** *a, b*) **rtl** : (
   int *n* = *num* **of** *a* * *num* **of** *b*,
     d = *den* **of** *a* * *den* **of** *b*;
   int *g* = *gcd* (n, d);

$$(n \div g, d \div g))$$

Since a structure display cannot be used as an operand, it is convenient to define an operator for constructing a rational from a pair of integers:

```
prior = 9;
op r = (int a, b) rtl : (
  int n := a, d := b;
  case sign d + 2
  in (n := −n; d := −d),
    (print ((newline, "illegal ⌣ rational")); stop)
  out skip
  esac;
  int g = gcd (n, d);
  (n ÷ g, d ÷ g))
```

Now division is most conveniently defined by

```
op / = (rtl a, b) rtl :
  a ∗ den of b r num of b
```

and the previous declaration of ∗ may be replaced by

```
op ∗ = (rtl a, b) rtl :
  (num of a ∗ num of b) r (den of a ∗ den of b)
```

Since the sum of p/q and s/t is $(pt + qs)/qt$, we have

```
op + = (rtl a, b) rtl :
  (num of a ∗ den of b + den of a ∗ num of b)
    r (den of a ∗ den of b)
```

and subtraction can then be defined in terms of this and the monadic − :

```
op − = (rtl a, b) rtl : a + −b
```

Many other operators with rational or mixed rational and integer operands can also be defined. Some more examples follow:

```
op abs = (rtl a) rtl : abs num of a r den of a,
  > = (rtl a, b) bool :
    num of a ∗ den of b > num of b ∗ den of a,
  plusab = (ref rtl a, rtl b) ref rtl : a := a + b,
```

timesab = (**ref rtl** a, **rtl** b) **ref rtl** : $a := a * b$,
$/$ = (**rtl** a, **int** b) **rtl** : $a * 1$ **r** b

Our set of rational operators could be improved through the use of extended precision for intermediate results as described in 6.6.1.

The simple problem described earlier may now be solved as follows:

rtl $a2, a1, a0,$ ¢ coefficients of first polynomial ¢
    $b2, b1, b0$; ¢ and of second polynomial ¢
$read ((a2, a1, a0, b2, b1, b0))$;
proc $print\ rtl\ sum$ = (**rtl** a, b) **void** : (
  rtl $c = a + b$;
  $print ((whole\ (num\ \textbf{of}\ c, 0),\ ''/'',$
    $whole(den\ \textbf{of}\ c, 0),\ ''\ldots''))\ )$;
$print\ rtl\ sum\ (a2, b2); print\ rtl\ sum\ (a1, b1)$;
$print\ rtl\ sum\ (a0, b0)$

Exercises

1. Declare an operator to raise a rational value to an integer power.
2. Using the operators defined in this section, define a procedure to compute (the coefficients of) the product of two quadratic polynomials.

6.4. Unions and Conformity Clauses

A UNION (or UNITED MODE) of a given set of modes is a derived mode where the values can be of any mode in the set. A declarer for such a mode consists of the symbol **union** followed by a parenthesized list of declarers for the contained modes. As an example, every value associated with the mode

    union (real, int)

has either the mode **real** or the mode **int**. United modes have some of the properties of sets, so that the above declarer could also be written as

    union (int, real)

In addition, the mode specified by

    union (bool, union (real, int))

is the same as

    union (bool, real, int)

To prevent ambiguities, not all combinations of modes are permitted within unions. In particular, a pair of modes cannot be so combined if one can be obtained from the other by the coercions of dereferencing and deproceduring. Thus

   union (int, ref int)

is invalid, in contrast to the valid mode

   union (int, [ ] int)

No bounds are included when a row mode appears in a union declarer.
   The variable declaration

   union (real, int) *ri*

generates a name of mode **ref union (real, int)** which may refer to either a real number or an integer. The primary purpose of unions is in fact to allow names where the modes of the values referred to may vary during execution. As with structures, a new symbol is often declared for the united mode, as in

   mode rent = union (real, int),
      brent = union (bool, real, int)

The new symbols can then be used in declarations:

   rent *ri1, ri2*;
   brent *bri1, bri2*

   The assignation

   ri1 := ri2

simply involves dereferencing *ri2* to **rent** and assigning the resulting real or integer value to *ri1*. The variable *ri2* might have acquired its value through an assignation such as

   ri2 := i + 15

where *i* is an integer variable. After the dereferencing of *i* and the addition, the value on the right of mode **int** formally undergoes the coercion of UNITING before being assigned to *ri2*. In general, uniting converts a given mode to some united mode containing it; in this case the resulting mode is **rent**, *i,e.,* **union(real,int)**. As a result, *ri2* refers to an integer value, but after the elaboration of

> *ri2* := *3.14*

it refers to a real value. In the case of

> *bri1* := *ri1*

ri1 is dereferenced to **rent** and then united to **brent (union(real,int)** to **union (bool,real,int))**.

It is possible for a union to include the mode **void**. The current mode can be set to **void** with the aid of a VOID DENOTATION, which consists of the symbol **empty**:

> **union (void, int)** *voint* := **empty**

This is the only use of the void denotation.

There are no predefined operators for any united modes, so that *ri1* + *ri2* is invalid. Operands can be united, however, so that if **opr** has been declared as an operator of mode **proc(brent,brent)brent**, then *ri1* **opr** *i* is a valid formula.

A united multiple can have any bounds, as long as it has an appropriate mode:

> **union ([ ]int, [ ]real)** *abc* := ([*n*] **int** *a*;
>   *read* (*a*); *a*)

The bounds of the current value of *abc* can be determined using the operators **upb** and **lwb**. If the union included a non-row mode, however, a formula such as **upb** *abc* would not be valid.

Since there is no 'deuniting' coercion, it is not possible to write an assignation such as

> *i* := *ri1*

even if it is known that *ri1* will refer to an integer. The desired effect is achieved by the unit

> **case** *ri1* **in (int** *j*) : *i* := *j* **esac**

which is a simple example of a CONFORMITY CLAUSE.

A conformity clause differs from a case clause in that it tests the mode of the series in the **case** part rather than its value. Each item in the **in** part has one of the following forms:

    (declarer) : unit
    (declarer identifier) : unit

Each declarer must specify a mode (possibly a subunion) contained in the united mode given by the **case** part. If one of the declarers specifies a mode which matches (i.e., is the same as or a union of) the actual mode, the unit which follows it is elaborated (but only one unit is elaborated if there is more than one match); otherwise, the **out** part, if any, is elaborated. If an identifier follows the declarer, it represents the 'deunited' value within the unit. Thus in the last example, *i*, which is global to the conformity clause, is assigned a new value if and only if *ri1* currently refers to an integer.

The following declaration defines a procedure which changes the mode of the value referred to by a **rent** name:

    proc *convert* = (**rent** *a*) **rent** :
      case *a*
      in (**int** *i*) : **real** (*i*),
          (**real** *x*) : **round** *x*
      esac

For the call in

    ri2 := *convert* (*ri2*)

we have the implicit identity declaration

    rent *a* = *ri2*

which has the effect of making *a* either a real constant or an integer constant, depending on the mode of the value of *ri2*. If *a* is an integer, the cast **real**(*i*) specifies that it is to be widened and a real value delivered. If *a* is real, it is rounded and an integer value delivered.

Exercises

1. Point out the errors in each of the following:
    (a) **mode abc** = **union** (**proc int**, **ref** [ ]**real**, **int**)
    (b) **mode def** = **union** (**bool**, [*5*] **bool**)
    (c) **int** *i* := (**union** (**int, real**) *ir* := *5*; *ir*)
    (d) (*un* | ([ ]**int** *a*) : *a*[*1*] := *5*, **void** : **skip** | *print*("?"))

2. Write a procedure with two **brent** parameters which delivers their sum if they are both numeric, the result of applying **and** to them if they are both Boolean, and an undefined value otherwise.

6.5 List Processing (SCO)

A 'linked list' is a set of values called the 'nodes' of the list, where each node generally includes information about how to access one or more other values related in some way to the given value. The term 'list processing' covers those programming techniques concerned with setting up and manipulating such data structures. The techniques are relevant to a broad range of non-numeric applications, including data processing, mathematical symbol manipulation, compiler writing, and artificial intelligence. A complete discussion of list processing is beyond the scope of this book, and we shall merely consider how some of the simpler techniques may be realized in Algol 68.

The simplest type of linked list is the linear list or 'chain', where each node except the last is linked to one other node, i.e., the next node in the chain. Each node can be represented by a structured value where one of the fields is the name of the next node:

mode node = **struct** ([*3*] **char** *info*, **ref node** *next*)

In this case, the non-linking information contained in each node is a single string value of length *3*. Although the mode declaration appears to be circular, it is valid because of the symbol **ref** in the *next* field. Now if we declare

node *p* := (*"abc"*, **nil**)

then the selection

next **of** *p*

has the mode **ref ref node**; i.e., it can be a pointer to another node. Its current value, however, is **nil** (mode **ref node**), indicating that *p* refers to the last (and the only) node in its chain. We may now define a second node and append it to the first:

node *q* := (*"def"*, **nil**);
next **of** *p* := *q*

Note that *q* is not dereferenced in the last statement. The following phrase adds a third node at the beginning of the chain:

node $r := ("ghi", p)$

The chain can now be pictured as follows:

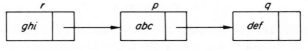

Figure 2   Example of a chain

The absence of an arrow leaving the *next* field of q corresponds to the name **nil**.

It is useful to have a variable for the entire chain, and this is best realized as a pointer to the first node, so that its mode is the same as that of the names of the *next* fields:

ref node $chn := r$

All the nodes can now be accessed through *chn*. The selection

info **of** *chn*

involves dereferencing *chn* and refers to *"ghi"*. The selection

next **of** *chn*

refers to the name p, so that

info **of** *next* **of** *chn*

refers to *"abc"*. Similarly,

info **of** *next* **of** *next* **of** *chn*

is the same as

info **of** q

and refers to *"def"*. The selection

info **of** *next* **of** q

is invalid because

ref node (*next* **of** *q*) **is nil**

is true, and **nil** never refers to any value.

For a long chain, it is undesirable to have to declare variables such as *p*, *q*, and *r* for the individual nodes. The following statement associates *chn* with the same chain as before without introducing these variables:

> *chn* := **heap node** :=
>   ("*ghi*",**heap node** :=
>   ("*abc*",**heap node** :=
>   ("*def*", **nil**)))

Note the use of global rather than local generators; this is usual in list processing since the creation and deletion of nodes generally takes place in an order different from that imposed by the clause structure of a program.

To remove a node from the chain, it is necessary to change the *next* field of the preceding node (or the value of *chn* if the first node is to be deleted) to be the name of the node following the one to be deleted (or **nil** if the last node is to be deleted). This name is in fact the *next* field of the node to be deleted. The change can be effected only by assignment to the name (mode **ref ref node**) of the *next* field of the previous node. Unless it is *chn*, this name does not have an identifier; we therefore arrange for it to be the value referred to by a variable *ptr* of mode **ref ref ref node**. The initial value of *ptr* will be *chn*, then the name of the *next* field of the first node, and so on until the node prior to the one to be deleted is reached. The following procedure deletes the *i*th node in a chain *chn*, where *i* must be between *1* and the length of the chain:

> **proc** *delete* = (**int** *i*, **ref ref node** *chn*) **void** : (
>   **ref ref node** *ptr* := *chn*;
>   **to** *i* − *1* **do** *ptr* := *next* **of** *ptr* **od**;
>   **ref ref node** (*ptr*) := *next* **of** *ptr*)

Note that in the selections *next* **of** *ptr*, *ptr* is dereferenced twice, and in the second case the name yielded by the selection is also dereferenced once.

The insertion of a node into a chain is somewhat similar except that the name assigned to the value of *ptr* is that yielded by a generator for the new node. The *next* field of the new node is the old *next* field to which *ptr* was pointing. In the following procedure, a node containing a string *s* is inserted after the *i*th existing node, where *i* ≥ *0*. If *i* is greater than the number of nodes, the new node goes at the end of the chain.

> **proc** *insert* = (**int** *i*, [ ] **char** *s*, **ref ref node** *chn*) **void** : (

```
      ref ref node ptr := chn;
      to i while ref node (ptr) isnt nil
         do ptr := next of ptr od;
      ref ref node (ptr) := heap node := (s, ptr) )
```

Another very important type of linked list is the 'binary tree', where each node is linked to zero, one, or two other nodes, and in general each node is associated with a left subtree and a right subtree. Binary trees can be used to store sets of strings in such a way that a given string can be located relatively quickly. The first string forms the 'root', the only node in the tree with no link from another node. If the second string lexicographically precedes (follows) the first string, then it forms a node which constitutes the left (right) subtree of the root. If the two strings are equal, no new node is created, but we may wish to record the number of occurrences of each string in the corresponding node, so that we have the mode declaration

mode btnode = struct (string *val*, int *num*,
                        ref btnode *left, right*)

Each distinct string forms a new 'leaf' of the tree, i.e., a node which as yet has no subtrees. Node scanning always begins at the root, and the string value at each node scanned determines whether the new node will be added to the left or to the right subtree of that node. Figure 3 shows the tree which is constructed for strings added in the order *frank, john, mary, sue, george, bill, cathy, mary*:

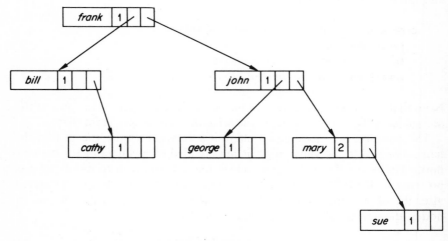

Figure 3   A binary tree

Given a pointer to the root, all the nodes in the tree can be accessed. Since there are initially no nodes at all, this pointer can be declared as

ref btnode *btree* := **nil**

Although a construction procedure could be programmed in a way analogous to the insertion procedure for chains, it is more convenient to use recursion:

```
proc update = (ref string s, ref ref btnode r) void :
  if ref btnode (r) is nil
  then r := heap btnode := (s, 1, nil nil)
  elif s < val of r
  then update (s, left of r)
  elif s > val of r
  then update (s, right of r)
  else num of r plusab 1
  fi
```

The procedure is initially called with the actual parameter *btree*; it then calls itself once for each level reached below the root. When a new node is added, it is again one of the linking fields (a name) of an existing node which is changed. The implicit identity declarations for r remove the need for a pointer of mode **ref ref ref btnode**.

The following procedure prints all the information in a tree such as *btree* according to the lexicographic order of the strings:

```
proc display = (ref ref btnode r) void :
  if ref btnode (r) isnt nil
  then display (left of r);
    print ((val of r, num of r, newline));
    display (right of r)
  fi
```

If recursion were not used in this case, the procedure would be considerably more complicated. The reader should verify that these procedures work for the example given above.

It is not always the case that all the nodes in a tree contain the same sort of information. Sometimes the leaf nodes are different from the others, as in the tree pictured in Figure 4, which could be used as a representation of the fully parenthesized symbolic expression

$$((x - a) + ((b + c) * z))$$

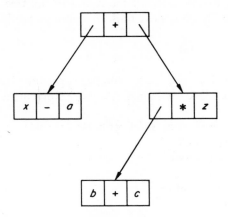

Figure 4   Tree representation of $((x-a) + ((b+c)*z))$

In such cases, united modes can be used in some of the fields of the nodes:

mode operand = **union** (**char**, **ref expr**);
mode expr = **struct** (**operand** *opd1*, **char** *opr*, **operand** *opd2*)

The following operator forms a tree representing the expression which is the symbolic product of two given expressions:

op * = (**operand** *a*, *b*) **operand** :
  heap expr := (*a*, *"*"*, *b*)

Note that the name yielded by the assignation is united to the mode **operand**. The following procedure will print any symbolic expression in fully parenthesized string form:

proc *print expr* = (**operand** *a*) **void** :
  case *a*
  in (**char** *c*) : *print* (*c*),
    (**ref expr** *e*) : (
      print (*"("*); *print expr* (*opd1* **of** *e*);
      print (*opr* **of** *e*); *print expr* (*opd2* **of** *e*);
      print (*")"*))
  esac

The value **nil** is not used in these lists, and the conformity clause takes over the function of the identity relations used in the previous examples.

Exercises

1. A chain represents a 'stack' if a new node always forms the head of the chain, in which case the stack is said to be 'pushed', and if the only node that is ever deleted is the current head, in which case the stack is said to be 'popped'. Using the mode **node** defined in this section, declare an operator ↓ to push a given string onto a stack and an operator ↑ to pop a stack and deliver the popped value.
2. Rewrite the procedure *update* without using recursion.
3. Write a procedure which delivers the 'reverse' of a given **operand** value. For example, the tree representing the fully parenthesized expression

$$((z * (c + b)) + (a - x))$$

would be produced from the one representing

$$((x - a) + ((b + c) * z))$$

6.6 Additional Numeric Modes

6.6.1 Nonstandard Precision

Sometimes it is desirable to have integer values greater than *max int* or real values with a higher precision than *real width* decimal digits (see 2.3.3). For this purpose, it is possible to construct new modes by prefixing the declarer **int** or **real** with one or more occurrences of the symbol **long**:

> **long int**
> **long real**
> **long long real**
> **long long long int**

The more **long** symbols there are, the greater the amount of storage used for a value of that mode; for example, a name of mode **ref int** might correspond to one machine word and one of mode **ref long int** to two words. There are also modes such as **short int**, **short real**, **short short int**, etc., where the values are represented in a smaller amount of storage than the standard.

In a given environment, only a certain number of these modes will be distinguished from all the others. The total number of integer (real) modes of a precision higher than or the same as the standard is given by the environment enquiry *int lengths* (*real lengths*). Similarly, the total number of integer (real) modes of a precision lower than or the same as the standard is given by the environment enquiry *int shorths* (*real shorths*). We shall hereafter assume that all of these are 2, so that, for example, **long long int** will not give us any more precision than **long int** and **short short int** will be equivalent to **short int**.

For each distinct integer and real mode, there are other environment enquiries corresponding to those given in 2.3.3. The ones for the modes we are considering are summarized in the following table:

Constant	Mode
int lengths	**int**
int shorths	**int**
real lengths	**int**
real shorths	**int**
long max int	**long int**
short max int	**short int**
long max real	**long real**
short max real	**short real**
long small real	**long real**
short small real	**short real**
long pi	**long real**
short pi	**short real**
long int width	**int**
short int width	**int**
long real width	**int**
short real width	**int**
long exp width	**int**
short exp width	**int**

The denotation for a long integer (long real) value consists of the corresponding integer (real) denotation preceded by **long**. (For a **long long** value, the denotation would contain two **long** symbols, and so on.) The denotation for a short integer (short real) value consists of the corresponding integer (real) denotation preceded by **short**. (For a **short short** value, the denotation would contain two **short** symbols, and so on.) Here are some declarations of variables and constants with values of nonstandard precision:

> **long int** *li, lj* := **long** *123456789*;
> **short int** *si, sj* := **short** *0*;
> **long real** *lx* = **long** *1.5e10*;
> **long real** *ly* := *li*

In the last phrase, the long integer value obtained by dereferencing *li* is widened to a long real value. A **short int** could similarly be widened to a **short real**. However, there are no coercions between integers or real numbers of different precisions. This function is provided by the monadic operators

leng ('lengthen') and **shorten** which are summarized below for the modes in which we are interested:

Symbols	Priority	Modes	
leng	*10*	**(int**	**) long int**
		(short int	**) int**
		(real	**) long real**
		(short real)	**real**
shorten	*10*	**(long int**	**) int**
		(int	**) short int**
		(long real	**) real**
		(real	**) short real**

Because the modes on the left and right sides do not match, the following assignations are invalid:

$$si := lj;$$
$$li := sj$$

The intended effect is achieved by

$$si := \textbf{shorten shorten } lj;$$
$$li := \textbf{leng leng } sj$$

The value of an operand of **shorten** should be small enough to be a value of the result mode.

All the arithmetic operators introduced previously are defined for operands of nonstandard precision, yielding results with the same level of precision. Thus we may write

$$li + \textbf{leng leng } si - \textbf{long } 1$$

but not

$$li + si - 1$$

because the operators are not defined for operands with different precisions. An exception is ↑, where the right operand always has the mode **int**.

The rules for transput of values with nonstandard precision are entirely analogous to those for standard precision; this applies to the material in the next chapter as well as to what has gone before. In the external data, the maximum numbers of digits in the values will be different than for standard precision, but the symbol **long** or **short** is never present. The first actual parameter in a call of *whole, fixed,* or *float* may have any precision.

As an example of the use of long integers, suppose that we wish to declare a monadic operator **mean** to find the average to the nearest integer of the elements of an integer multiple. Although the mode of the operator is to be **proc(ref [ ]int)int**, the sum of the elements, which is an intermediate result in the calculation, may exceed *max int*, especially if several of the elements are very large. The operator is therefore declared as follows:

```
op mean = (ref [] int a) int : (
    long int sum := long 0;
    for i from lwb a to upb a
        do sum plusab leng a[i] od;
    shorten round (sum / leng upb a[at 1]) )
```

Exercises

1. Declare addition operators for mixed **int** and **long int** operands.
2. Using the mode **union (short int, int, long int)**, write a procedure which delivers the factorial of an **int** in the shortest possible precision.

6.6.2 Precise Numeric Calculations (NUM)

Predefined mathematical procedures corresponding to those introduced in 2.3.5 are available for all the nonstandard real modes. For example, *long sqrt* has the mode **proc(long real) long real** and *short sqrt* is a **proc(short real) short real**. Similarly, we have *long random* of mode **proc long real** and *short random* of mode **proc short real**.

The problem of when extended precision should be used is largely a question of numerical analysis and so is beyond the scope of this book. It turns out that one situation where it may be necessary is in the calculation of sums of products in matrix multiplication. The operator given in 5.5 could thus be redefined as follows:

```
op * = (ref [,] real a, b) ref [,] real :
    if int m = 1 upb a, n = 2 upb a, p = 2 upb b;
        1 lwb a = 1 and 2 lwb a = 1 and 1 lwb b = 1
        and 2 lwb b = 1 and 1 upb b = n
    then heap [m,p] real c;
        long real cij;
        for i to m do
            ref [ ] real arow = a[i,];
            for j to p do
```

```
            ref [ ] real bcol  =  b[,j];
            cij := long 0;
            for k to n do
                cij plusab leng arow[k] * leng bcol[k] od;
            c[i,j] := shorten cij
        od
    od;
    c
fi
```

In some circumstances it may be convenient to declare one procedure which will work regardless of the precision of the actual parameters. Given the mode declaration

mode realno = union (real, long real)

the following procedure computes the value of

$$\sqrt{x^2 + y^2}$$

where the modes of x and y may be either **real** or **long real** :

```
proc root of squares  =  (realno a, b)  realno :
    case a
    in (real x):
        case b
        in (real y) :
            sqrt (x * x  +  y * y),
            (long real ly):
            long sqrt (leng (x * x)  +  ly * ly)
        esac,
    (long real lx) :
        case b
        in (real y) :
            long sqrt (lx * lx  +  leng (y * y)),
            (long real ly) :
            long sqrt (lx * lx  +  ly * ly)
        esac
    esac
```

Note that the result is of mode **long real** if at least one of the parameters is.

Exercises

1. Write a procedure to approximate e^x by summing an infinite series (see 4.4.3) and using extended precision for intermediate results.
2. Write a procedure which delivers, in the same precision, the natural logarithm of a **real**, **long real**, or **short real**.

6.6.3 Complex Arithmetic (NUM)

Mathematically, a complex number is an ordered pair (x,y) of real numbers, where x is interpreted as the 'real' part and y as the 'imaginary' part. Such a number can also be expressed as the sum of the two parts, where the imaginary part has been multiplied by i, the square root of -1:

$$x + iy$$

In Algol 68, the mode **compl** is predefined as

> **mode compl** = **struct** (**real** *re, im*)

Thus a structure display such as (*1.2*, *3.4*) may represent a complex value. There is also a dyadic operator **i** or⊥,of priority *9*, which yields a complex value given two real numbers or integers, so that *1.2* **i** *3.4* means the same thing but can be used in more contexts.

    If we have

> **compl** *z1* := *1.2* **i** *3.4, z2*

then clearly *re* **of** *z1* refers to *1.2* and *im* **of** *z1* refers to *3.4*. These values are also yielded by the formulas **re** *z1* and **im** *z1*, because the monadic operators **re** and **im** are predefined as follows:

> **op re** = (**compl** *a*) **real** : *re* **of** *a*;
> **op im** = (**compl** *a*) **real** : *im* **of** *a*

Note that

> **re** *z2* := **im** *z1*

is illegal but can be replaced by

> *re* **of** *z2* := **im** *z1*

The assignation

$z2 := z1$

changes both fields of $z2$ to the corresponding values in $z1$. There is a widening coercion from **real** to **compl**, so that

$z2 := 5.6$

is valid and equivalent to

$z2 := 5.6$ **i** 0

In the case of

$z2 := 5$

The integer 5 is widened twice, first to **real** and then to **compl**.

All the usual arithmetic operators are defined for complex operands and for combinations with integer and real operands. In addition, the 'conjugate' of a complex number is obtained using the predefined monadic operator

op conj $=$ (**comp** a) **compl** : **re** a **i** $-$**im** a

and its 'modulus' is yielded by the predefined operator

op abs $=$ (**compl** a) **real** : $sqrt$ (**re** $a \uparrow 2$ $+$ **im** $a \uparrow 2$)

The operator **arg** is predefined as follows:

```
op arg  =  (compl a) real :
   if real re  =  re a, im  =  im a;
      re ≠ 0 or im ≠ 0
   then if abs re > abs im
      then arc tan (im/re)  +  pi/2 *
          (im < 0 | sign re  −  1 | 1  −  sign re)
      else  −  arc tan (re/im)  +  pi/2 * sign im
      fi
   fi
```

For readers unfamiliar with the standard rules for complex arithmetic, here are the definitions of addition, multiplication, and division of pairs of complex numbers:

op $+$ $=$ (**compl** a, b) **compl** :

$$(\mathbf{re}\ a\ +\ \mathbf{re}\ b)\ \mathbf{i}\ (\mathbf{im}\ a\ +\ \mathbf{im}\ b);$$

op * = (**compl** a, b) **compl** :
$$(\mathbf{re}\ a * \mathbf{re}\ b\ -\ \mathbf{im}\ a * \mathbf{im}\ b)\ \mathbf{i}$$
$$(\mathbf{re}\ a * \mathbf{im}\ b\ +\ \mathbf{im}\ a * \mathbf{re}\ b);$$

op / = (**compl** a, b) **compl** : (
  real d = **re** (b * **conj** b);
  compl n = a * **conj** b;
  $(\mathbf{re}\ n\ /\ d)\ \mathbf{i}\ (\mathbf{im}\ n\ /\ d)\ )$

Complex values can also have nonstandard precision; the mode **long compl**, for example, is equivalent to

struct (**long real** *re, im*)

The number of distinct precisions of complex values available in an implementation is the same as that for real values, and each mode has its full complement of operators.

All the predefined operators involving complex values are summarized in the following table. For operands with nonstandard precision, only **leng** and **shorten** are listed.

Symbols			Priority	Modes
plusab	+:=		*1*	(**ref compl, compl**) **ref compl**
				(**ref compl, int**) **ref compl**
				(**ref compl, real**) **ref compl**
minusab	− :=		*1*	as for **plusab**
timesab	* :=	× :=	*1*	as for **plusab**
divab	/ :=		*1*	as for **plusab**
=	**eq**		*4*	(**compl, compl**) **bool**
				(**compl, int**) **bool**
				(**compl, real**) **bool**
				(**int, compl**) **bool**
				(**real, compl**) **bool**
≠	/=	**ne**	*4*	as for =
+			*6*	(**compl, compl**) **bool**
				(**compl, int**) **compl**
				(**compl, real**) **compl**
				(**int, compl**) **compl**
				(**real, compl**) **compl**
−			*6*	as for +
*	×		*7*	as for +
/			*7*	as for +

Symbols	Priority	Modes	
↑ ** up	8	(compl, int	) compl
i	9	(real, real	) compl
		(int, int	) compl
		(int, real	) compl
		(real, int	) compl
+	10	(compl	) compl
−	10	(compl	) compl
re	10	(compl	) real
im	10	(compl	) real
conj	10	(compl	) compl
abs	10	(compl	) real
arg	10	(compl	) real
leng	10	(compl	) long compl
		(short compl	) compl
shorten	10	(long compl	) compl
		(compl	) short compl

When complex values are transput, the character ⊥ or the letter *i* is inserted or expected in the external data between the two real values; it may be preceded or followed by spaces. On input, a real value will not be widened to **compl**. Although it is a structure, a complex value is never straightened, so that both fields must appear on the same line in simple output. Of course this is not so if the complex variable in the transput statement is replaced by the selections for the fields, in which case ⊥ or *i* will not appear externally.

As a simple example of the use of the complex mode, consider the mathematical square root function. When its argument is negative the result is an imaginary number, i.e., a complex number with a real part of *0*. The function can therefore be defined as follows:

```
proc sqrtc = (real a) compl :
  if a ≥ 0
  then sqrt (a) i 0
  else 0 i sqrt (−a)
  fi
```

This procedure is used in the following sequence, where *a*, *b*, and *c* are assumed to yield the real coefficients of a quadratic equation. If the roots are real values, they are printed as such; otherwise, the complex roots are printed.

```
real a2 = 2 * a;
compl d = sqrtc (b * c − 4 * a * c);
compl x1 = (−b + d) / a2,
     x2 = (−b − d) / a2;
```

```
if im x1 = 0
then print ((re x1, re x2))
else print ((x1, x2))
fi
```

A procedure to compute the square root (with nonnegative real part) of a complex number can be declared as follows:

```
proc csqrt = (compl z) compl : (
    real x = re z, y = im z;
    real rp = sqrt ((abs x + sqrt (x * x + y * y)) /2);
    real ip = (rp = 0 | 0 | y/(2 * rp));
    if x ≥ 0 then rp i ip else abs ip i ( y ≥ 0 | rp | −rp) fi )
```

Exercises

1. Write a procedure to calculate the exponential of a complex value, given the equation

$$e^{a+ib} = e^a (\cos b + i \sin b)$$

2. Write a procedure to print a table of values of any given complex function of one argument, where the values for the argument are contained in a complex multiple. Use it to tabulate e^{x+iy} for all integer values of x and y between -2 and 2.

6.7 Manipulation of Machine Words (SCO)

In some applications it is desirable to have access to the actual words of the computer's memory, either for reasons of efficiency or because of the very nature of the application (e.g., systems programming). Such applications are rather advanced, and this section simply describes the relevant language features without considering their practical use.

A value of mode **bits** is essentially a machine word considered as a sequence of values of mode **bool**, and **bytes** a machine word considered as a sequence of **char** values. The number of Boolean values in a **bits** value is given by the environment enquiry *bits width*, and the number of characters in a **bytes** value is given by *bytes width*. There are also long and short versions of these modes. A **long bits** value contains *long bits width* Boolean values, and so on. The number of distinct **bits** modes of width not less than the standard is given by the environment enquiry *bits lengths*, and the number of widths not greater than the standard is given by *bits shorths*. Similarly, there are environment enquiries *bytes lengths* and *bytes shorths* for the **bytes** modes.

A denotation for a **bits** value has the form

radix *r* digit-sequence

Where the redix is either *2*, *4*, *8*, or *16*, and the digits following the letter *r* are appropriate to that radix. For a radix of *16*, the extra digits are represented by the letters *a* through *f*. The following denotations are all equivalent:

2 r 101010011111	(binary)
4 r 222133	(quaternary)
8 r 5237	(octal)
16 r a9f	(hexadecimal)

In the binary notation, *1* corresponds to **true** and *0* to **false**. The value of *bits width* must not be less than *12* in this case; if it is greater than *12*, the value will automatically be padded on the left with **false**'s. A denotation for a **long bits (short bits)** value begins with the symbol **long (short)**, so that we might have the following declarations:

bits *bi* := *8r777*;
long bits *lbi* := **long** *8r77*;
short bits *sbi* := **short** *8r7777*

The total length of the value of *sbi* is *short bits width*, which must be at least *12*.

There are no denotations for **bytes** values, but a string of length not greater than *bytes width* can be converted to a **bytes** using the predefined procedure *bytes pack* of mode **proc(string)bytes**:

bytes *by* := *bytes pack* (*"abcd"*)

If *bytes width* is greater than *4*, the value of *by* will be padded on the right with an appropriate number of instances of some character, perhaps blanks, given by the environment enquiry *null character*. For **long bytes**, the conversion procedure is *long bytes pack*, and so forth:

long bytes *lby* := *long bytes pack* (*"pq"*);
short bytes *sby* := *short bytes pack* (*"xyz"*)

There are two more varieties of the widening coercion: a **bits** can be widened to a multiple with mode and bounds [*1*: *bits width*] **bool**, and a **bytes** can be widened to a string with *bytes width* characters. The long and short versions can be widened in an analogous way. The modes obtained by widening should not be confused with such modes as [ ] **bits** and [ ] **bytes**.

Several operators are available for the manipulation of **bits** values and their long and short versions. The monadic operator **not** reverses each element in its operand, so that if *bits width* is *16*, then **not** *16ra9f* yields

   2r1111010101100000

which can also be written as

   16rf560

The result of applying the dyadic operator **and** to a pair of (**long, short**) **bits** operands is a (**long, short**) **bits** value where each element is the result of applying **and** to the corresponding elements of the operands. Thus

   2r101 **and** *2r110*

yields *2r100*. The operator **or** is defined in a corresponding manner.

The monadic operator **bin** converts a nonnegative (long, short) integer to the (**long, short**) **bits** value corresponding to the binary representation of the integer; conversely, **abs** converts a (**long, short**) **bits** to a (long, short) integer. The comparison operators = and ≠ can be applied to (**long, short**) **bits** operands as if **abs** had first been applied to each operand; ≤ delivers **true** if each **true** in the left value corresponds to a **true** in the right value, and ≥ has a corresponding meaning. The operator **elem** or ⌷, of priority 7, takes an integer operand i on the left and a (**long, short**) **bits** operand b on the right and delivers the Boolean value at the ith position in b. The result of applying **shl**,↑, or **up** to a (**long, short**) **bits** operand b on the left and an integer operand i on the right is the (**long, short**) **bits** value obtained by shifting the elements of b by i places, to the left if i is positive and to the right if i is negative, padding with **false**'s. The operator **shr**,↓, or **down** causes a shift in the opposite direction. Thus the following expressions are all equivalent:

   2r10100
   2r101 **shl** *2*
   2r101 **shr** *−2*
   2r1010010 **shr** *2*
   2r1010010 **shl** *−2*

The procedure *bits pack*, of mode **proc([]bool)bits**, converts a Boolean multiple with not more than *bits width* elements to a **bits** value, padding with **false**'s on the left. Similarly, we have *long bits pack* of mode **proc([]bool) long bits**, *short bits pack* of mode **proc([]bool) short bits**, and so on. There are also a number of predefined lengthening and shortening operators such as the following:

op leng = (**bits** *a*) **long bits** : *long bits pack* (*a*);
op shorten = (**long bits** *a*) **bits** :
   bits pack([ ]**bool** (*a*) [*long bits width* − *bits width* + *1* :])

When the right operand of **elem** is a (**long, short**) **bytes** value, the result is the *i*th character in the value. All six comparison operators can be used with **bytes** operands, and the effect is similar to that with string operands. It is worth nothing that since operands cannot be widened and + is not defined for **bytes** operands,

   string *s* := *"abc"* + *by2*

is invalid; it can be replaced by

   string *s* := *"abc"* + **string** (*by2*)

The following are examples of the definitions of **leng** and **shorten** for the **bytes** modes:

op leng = (**bytes** *a*) **long bytes** : *long bytes pack* (*a*);
op shorten = (**long bytes** *a*) **bytes** :
   bytes pack (**string** (*a*) [: *bytes width*])

All the above operators are summarized in the following table; those involving long or short values, except for **leng** and **shorten**, are omitted.

Symbols			Priority	Modes	
or	∨		2	(**bits**, **bits**	) **bits**
and	∧		3	(**bits**, **bits**	) **bits**
=	**eq**		4	(**bits**, **bits**	) **bool**
				(**bytes**, **bytes**	) **bool**
≠	/=	**ne**	4	as for =	
≤	<=	**le**	5	as for =	
≥	>=	**ge**	5	as for =	
<	**lt**		5	(**bytes**, **bytes**	) **bool**
>	**gt**		5	(**bytes**, **bytes**	) **bool**
elem	▯		7	(**int**, **bits**	) **bool**
				(**int**, **bytes**	) **char**
shl	↑	**up**	8	(**bits**, **int**	) **bits**

Symbols	Priority	Modes		
shr ↓ **down**	*8*	(**bits**,	**int**	) **bits**
not ⌐ ~	*10*	(**bits**		) **bits**
abs	*10*	(**bits**		) **int**
bin	*10*	(**int**		) **bits**
leng	*10*	(**bits**		) **long bits**
		(**short bits**		) **bits**
		(**bytes**		) **long bytes**
		(**short bytes**) **bytes**		
shorten	*10*	(**bits**		) **short bits**
		(**long bits**		) **bits**
		(**bytes**		) **short bytes**
		(**long bytes**) **bytes**		

For purposes of transput, **bytes** is treated like [ ]**char** and **bits** is treated like [ ]**bool**.

Chapter 7
Transput

In previous chapters, programs have been able to read only from the standard input device and to write only to the standard output device. Moreover, only FORMATLESS transput has been used, which means that the external data and its layout have been subject to various restrictive rules for the sake of convenience. In this chapter we consider the use of other peripheral devices (7.1) using both formatless (7.2) and FORMATTED (7.3) transput, the latter providing the programmer with a much greater degree of control over the appearance and layout of data. Still more control is provided by certain auxiliary facilities (7.4) for handling errors and other special conditions arising from transput operations. Finally, there is a third form of transput (7.5) which can be used for the efficient handling of data on a secondary storage medium.

7.1 The Organization of Data

7.1.1 Books, Channels, and Files

A BOOK is a set of data on some external medium, such as cards or magnetic tape, which can be accessed by an Algol 68 program. A book consists of a sequence of characters, where the characters are organized into lines, and the lines are further organized into pages. Thus a position in the book may be considered as a triple (p, l, c), where p is the page number, l is the line number within the page, and c is the character number within the line. The LOGICAL END of a book is the first position following the last item of data; the logical end of an empty book is the position $(1, 1, 1)$. Finally, a book may have an IDENTIFICATION, i.e., a title, label, or 'password' which distinguishes it from other books. In some cases the identification can be changed by a program.

A CHANNEL is a means by which a program can access books and corresponds to one or more peripheral devices. Each available channel in the environment is represented within a program by a unique structured value, of the special mode **channel**, for which there should be an environment enquiry. Three of these constants, *stand in channel, stand out channel,* and *stand back channel,* respectively represent the standard input channel (e.g., a card reader), the standard output channel (e.g., a lineprinter), and the standard backup channel (e.g., a disk). The latter can be used for the temporary storage of data which is to be re-input later by the same or by a different program.

A book may be referred to within a program by a field of a structured value with the special mode **file** . The field selectors for the mode **file** as well as for **channel** are not available to the programmer. Names of mode **ref file** can be created in the usual way:

>   **file** *in2, out2*

To make a file refer to a book via some channel, i.e., to OPEN the file, it is necessary to call one of the predefined procedures *open, establish,* and *create.* The mode of *open* is **proc(ref file,string,channel)int**, and this procedure is used when the file referred to by the first actual parameter is to be linked with a book which already exists:

>   *open (in2, "book1", tape channel)*

The parameter *"book1"* specifies the book's identification, and *tape channel* is assumed to be an environment enquiry for the channel through which the book is to be accessed. If the second parameter were the empty string, some default book would be sought.

To open a new, empty book, the procedure *establish,* of mode **proc(ref file,string,channel,int,int,int)int** can be called:

>   *establish (out2, "book2", disk channel, 1000, 100, 200)*

Here *"book2"* is the identification and *disk channel* is assumed to represent the channel number for the new book. The third, fourth, and fifth parameters specify the number of pages, number of lines per page, and number of characters per line in the book. The call will succeed only if the call

>   *estab possible (disk channel)*

would yield **true**, where *estab possible* is a predefined procedure of mode **proc(channel)bool**. If the book is to have the default numbers of pages, lines, and characters for the channel, the procedure *create,* of mode **proc(ref file, channel)int**, can be used instead of *establish*:

create (out2, disk channel)

All these procedures deliver *0* if opening is successful.

There are three predefined file variables, *stand in*, *stand out*, and *stand back*, which are already open at the beginning of a program and which refer to their respective books via *stand in channel*, *stand out channel*, and *stand back channel*.

Once a file has been opened, data can be read from or written to the corresponding book by means of the facilities described in the remaining sections of this chapter. When a book is no longer needed by the program, the file should be CLOSED (i.e., dissociated from its book and channel) by a call of one of the predefined procedures *close*, *lock*, and *scratch*, all of which have the mode **proc(ref file)void**:

close (out2)

Depending on the implementation, these procedures could differ from each other as follows: when *close* is used, the book may again become accessible later in the program when another file is opened; when *lock* is used, the book remains intact but cannot be accessed again during the current elaboration of the program; *scratch* causes the destruction of the book, freeing the external storage for other purposes. The three standard files are locked automatically upon termination of the program.

When a file is open, the possible means of accessing its book can be determined by calling various predefined procedures with the mode **proc (ref file)bool**. If f is a file variable, *get possible* (f) yields **true** if the book, the channel, and perhaps other factors are suitable for input operations; *put possible* (f) yields **true** if output is possible, *bin possible* (f) if binary transput (7.5) is possible, and *compressible* (f) if the pages may have a variable number of lines and the lines a variable number of characters. We have *reset possible* (f) if the program can reset the current position to $(1, 1, 1)$ (by rewinding a magnetic tape, for example) and *set possible* (f) if the program can set the current position to any valid value; in the latter case, the book is called a RANDOM ACCESS book, meaning that programs are not required to transput the data in the order in which it appears in the book.

The call *reidf possible* (f) yields **true** if the book's identification can be changed. If this is the case, such a change can be effected by calling the procedure *reidf*, of mode **proc(ref file,string)void**:

reidf (in2, "book3")

The following table shows the minimal capabilities of the three standard files. The vacant entries are determined only by the implementation.

	stand in	*stand out*	*stand back*
get possible	**true**		**true**
put possible		**true**	**true**
bin possible			**true**
compressible			
reset possible			**true**
set possible			**true**
reidf possible			

7.1.2 Internal Books

It is possible to use a variable of mode **ref[ ]char**, **ref[ ][ ]char**, or **ref[ ]** **[ ][ ]char** as a book. If we have the declarations

> [*1000*] **char** *bk1*;
> [*30*] [*80*] **char** *bk2*;
> [*5*] [*50*] [*120*] **char** *bk3*

then *bk1* might represent a book of *1000* characters not divided into lines or pages, *bk2* a book of *30* lines, each containing *80* characters, and *bk3* a book of *5* pages, each containing *50* lines, each containing *120* characters. Transput to or from such internal books does not involve the use of a physical channel.

A file referred to by *f* can be opened on an internal book only by calling the procedure *associate*, of mode **proc(ref file,ref[ ][ ][ ]char)void**:

> *associate* (*f, bk2*)

(In this case, *bk2* will be rowed to **ref[ ][ ][ ]char** with bounds [*1 : 1*] [*1 :30*] [*1 :80*].) The properties of the internal book can be summarized as follows:

get possible (*f*)	**not** *bin possible* (*f*)
put possible (*f*)	**not** *compressible* (*f*)
reset possible (*f*)	**not** *reidf possible* (*f*)
set possible (*f*)	

We thus have a convenient facility for setting up random access books. When all transput operations are complete, the file may be closed.

7.2 Formatless Transput

The principal procedure for formatless input is *get*, which has two formal parameters. In a call, the first actual parameter specifies the name of some open file *f* where *get possible* (*f*) would yield **true**, and the second parameter is either a unit or a row display with any number of elements. The procedure *read* can be used instead of *get* for the standard input file, so that the following forms are equivalent:

> *read* (data-list)
> *get* (*stand in*, data-list)

The mode yielded by each item in the data list must be either **proc(ref file)void**, which is the mode of some layout procedures, or **ref** M, where M is any mode other than that of a union, routine, another name, or a multiple or structure containing any of these. The rules regarding layout of data for the various permitted modes have already been described in earlier chapters; there are no differences here between *get* and *read* apart from those imposed by differing line and page sizes.

The output procedure corresponding to *get* is *put*. The first actual parameter specifies the name of an open file *f* where *put possible* (*f*) would yield **true**. For the standard output file, *print* or *write* may be used instead, so that the following forms are equivalent:

> *print* (data-list)
> *write* (data-list)
> *put* (*stand out*, data-list)

In this case, each item in the data list must yield either a **proc(ref file)void** or any other value which is not a union, routine, name, or a multiple or structure containing any of these. Again, the standard layout rules have been described elsewhere.

The predefined layout identifiers *newpage*, *newline*, *space*, and *backspace* all have the mode **proc(ref file)void**, so that they may appear in data lists as described in 2.2.2 for the case of *print*. When used with *get* or *read*, *space* causes one character of data to be ignored, *newline* (*newpage*) causes the rest of the current line (page) to be ignored, and *backspace* moves the current position back one character (but not past the beginning of the current line), so that on input the character can be read a second time and on output it can be replaced by another character.

These procedures can also be called explicitly; for example, *newpage* (*standout*) starts a new printed page, and *backspace* (*f*) backspaces a file referred to by *f*. The following is a declaration of a procedure for skipping any number *n* of characters of the book referred to by any file *f*:

> **proc** *nspace* = (**ref file** *f*, **int** *n*) **void** :
>   **to** *n* **do** *space* (*f*) **od**

There is an additional predefined procedure *set char number*, of mode **proc(ref file, int)void**, which changes the position within the current line as specified by the second parameter.

Since *close*, *lock*, and *scratch* have the mode **proc(ref file)void**, they could also appear without parameters in data lists:

  put (*f*, (*i, j, k, close*))

Naturally this makes sense only when the procedure identifier is the last item in the list.

An open file referred to by *f* which is such that *reset possible* (*f*) yields **true** can be returned to the position (*1, 1, 1*) by the statement *reset* (*f*). This procedure is also a **proc(ref file)void**, so that *get* (*f, reset*) (assuming *get possible* (*f*)) or *put* (*f, reset*) (assuming *put possible* (*f*)) has the same effect.

If *f* is linked to a random access book (*set possible* (*f*)), then it can be set to any position (*i, j, k*) by the statement

  set (*f, i, j, k*)

where *set* has the mode **proc(ref file, int, int, int)void**.

As a simplified illustration of the use of some of these facilities, suppose that we have on disk a very large number of data records, each consisting of one integer and two real numbers. We require a program which will update this information from time to time and aid in maintaining the accuracy of the information. The update commands take the form of data cards, where the first number on a card is either *1*, to indicate a verification operation, or *2*, to indicate a replacement operation; the next three numbers give the position of the record, and the last three are the record values to be used in the verification or replacement. In the following program, it is assumed that *disk channel* is an environment enquiry and that the number of commands is given on the first card:

```
begin
    int n, type, page, line, char;
    struct (int v1, real v2, v3) record1, record2;
    file database; open (database, " ", disk channel);
    read (n);
    to n do
        read ((type, page, line, char, record1));
        print ((case type in "verify ̲ ", "replace"
            out " ???????" esac, " ̲ at ̲ ",
```

```
        page, line, char, " ⌣⌣ ", record1, newline));
    set (database, page, line, char);
    case type
    in (get (database, record2);
        if v1 of record1 ≠ v1 of record 2 or
           v2 of record1 ≠ v2 of record2 or
           v3 of record1 ≠ v3 of record2
        then print (("error ⌣ in ⌣ record:",
                        record2, newline))
        fi ),
        put (database, record1)
    out print (("invalid ⌣ update ⌣ type", newline))
    esac
  od ;
  close (database)
end
```

7.3 Formatted Transput

7.3.1 Formats

A value of mode **format**, which is a special structure mode, provides a detailed specification of the layout of data to be transput. Names of formats can be generated by declarations such as

   format *fmt1*, *fmt2*

and new modes involving **format** can be constructed in all the usual ways. However, format values cannot be transput. This rather long section is concerned only with the specification of formats; statements which actually carry out formatted transput are described in 7.3.2.

A format is represented within a program by a FORMAT TEXT, which is delimited by two $ symbols and contains a list of one or more PICTURES separated by commas. In the simplest case, each picture regulates the transput of a single value by means of constituents called FRAMES, the various types of which are described below. As auxiliary layout information, a picture may also include any number of INSERTIONS before, after, or between frames. A picture may consist entirely of insertions, in which case it does not regulate the transput of a value. The frames and insertions within a picture are strung together without any delimiting symbols.

The insertion *x* is equivalent to a call of *space* for the relevant file at the time transput takes place. Similarly, *y*, *l*, and *p* correspond to calls of *backspace*, *newline*, and *newpage*, respectively. The insertion *q* is like *x*, except that the skipped character is always a blank. A string or character denotation may also be used as an insertion; on output, the string will be printed, and on input the incoming characters must match the string. In the following format text, the first and only picture contains only insertions and specifies that a new page is to be begun, that the string *"heading"* is to be output or expected as input, and that a new line is to be begun:

$p "heading" l$

7.3.1.1 Frames

A format should account for every character in the data stream, regardless of the modes of the corresponding values within the program. For values of any numeric mode, the letter d represents a DIGIT FRAME, i.e., a frame corresponding to a single decimal digit in the external representation of a number. Thus dd could be a picture, containing two frames, for a two-digit integer, and $d\,q\,d$ a picture, containing two frames and an insertion, for an integer with a space between its two digits. A ZERO FRAME (z) is the same as a digit frame except that if the digit is a zero it is replaced (or expected to be replaced) by a space. For example, the picture zd is consistent with 25 or 5 but not 05.

In addition to digit or zero frames, a picture for a real value must contain either a POINT FRAME (.) or an EXPONENT FRAME (e) or both. A point frame indicates that a decimal point is to be output or expected, and an exponent frame indicates that an exponent symbol ($e,\backslash,\text{or}_{10}$) is to be output or expected. Thus $d.d$ could be a picture for a real number with one digit on each side of the decimal point, and $d.dxed$ would indicate that these are to be followed by a space, an exponent symbol, and a single-digit exponent. For complex values, which were introduced in 6.6.3, the frames for the two constituent real values are separated by a COMPLEX FRAME (i), indicating that $\perp$ or i is to be output or expected.

All of the frames mentioned so far may be preceded by an s, indicating that the character will not actually be transput but that everything is to continue as if it had been. On input, the frame sd corresponds to the implicit input of a zero, although the current position in the data is not advanced. As an example of this facility, the picture $ds.d$ could be used for the input of the real value 5.6 which appears externally as 56.

The SIGN FRAME + indicates that one of the sign characters + or − is to be output or expected; − is another sign frame signifying that either a space or − is to be output or expected. Sign frames may appear only just before the zero or digit frame for the leading digit of a number or an exponent. Two additional sign frames are introduced below.

For Boolean values, a BOOLEAN FRAME (b) indicates that T or F is to be output or expected. A Boolean frame must be the only frame in its picture. Additional frames involving non-numeric data will be introduced in 7.3.3.

7.3.1.2 *Replicators*

To save writing, insertions and some frames can be preceded by REPLICA-TORS, which in the simplest case are integer denotations. A replicator signifies that the insertion or frame following it is to be repeated that number of times. Thus the format text

$$\$\, p\, "*****"\, xxxxx\ -dddd,\, xxx\ -zd.ddde + zd\, \$$$

can be written more concisely as

$$\$\, p\, 5\, "*"\, 5x\ -4d,\, 3x\ -zd.3de + zd\, \$$$

A replicated zero frame indicates that only leading zeros are to be replaced by spaces, so that $3z$ is consistent with$-$ 22 and 202 but not 022.

All the insertions introduced previously can be replicated. An additional type of insertion (k) is always used with a replicator which corresponds to the second parameter in a call of *set char number*. As an example, the following format specifies that three integers are to begin in positions within a line which are multiples of *20*:

$$\$\, l\, 5d,\, 20k\, 5d,\, 40k\, 5d\, \$$$

Digit and zero frames are the only frames introduced so far which can be replicated. There are two additional sign frames, represented by $z+$ and $z-$, which in practice are always used with replicators. If R represents some integer denotation, then the frame $Rz+$ is similar to Rz except that $+$ or $-$ is output or expected immediately before the first digit, and $Rz-$ is similar to Rz except that a space or $-$ is to appear just before the first digit. Thus the picture $3z+d$ is consistent with any of the following:

```
+1234
 +34
 -4
 +0
```

Note that with the picture $+3zd$, these numbers would appear as

```
+1234
+  34
```

```
-    4
+    0
```

A replicator can also be applied to a parenthesized COLLECTION of one or more pictures. As an example, the format text

$$ \$ \; 4(-6zd, 4x \; b \; 4x), 2z - .3d \; \$ $$

is equivalent to the following expanded version:

$$ \$ \; -6zd, 4x \; b \; 4x, \; -6zd, 4x \; b \; 4x, \; -6zd, 4x \; b \; 4x, $$
$$ -6zd, 4x \; b \; 4\text{x}, 2z - .3d \; \$ $$

Replicated collections can be nested in this way to any depth and may be preceded or followed by insertions. As a second example,

$$ \$ \; 2(3 \; "a" \; 3(3d \; x) \; l) \; \$ $$

is equivalent to

$$ \$ \; 3 \; "a" \; 3d \; x, 3d \; x, 3d \; x \; l, 3 \; "a" \; 3d \; x, 3d \; x, 3d \; x \; l \; \$ $$

Sometimes a replicator cannot be expressed as an integer denotation because its value is not known until the program is elaborated. In such cases we must use an enclosed clause which yields an integer value and is preceded by the letter n. If i is an integer variable, for example, the format text

$$ \$ \; 3d, n(i) \; (l \; 2x \; 4z + d \; 2x, 2z + .2d) \; \$ $$

could be the same as any of the following depending on the value of i:

$$ \$ \; 3d \; \$ $$
$$ \$ \; 3d, l \; 2x \; 4z + d \; 2x, 2z + .2d \; \$ $$
$$ \$ \; 3d, l \; 2x \; 4z + d \; 2x, 2z + .2d, l \; 2x \; 4z + d \; 2x, 2z + .2d \; \$ $$
etc.

This format could be used for the transput of an integer followed by a multiple declared as

$$ [1:i] \; \textbf{struct} \; (\textbf{int} \; a, \textbf{real} \; b) \; c $$

It should also be noted that the format could not be assigned to a format name with a larger scope than i.

7.3.1.3 Special Types of Picture

There are three other types of picture which may begin and end with insertions but which contain no frames.

A FORMAT PICTURE contains the letter f followed by an enclosed clause yielding a format. It may be used in such a way that part or all of a format is fixed only when transput actually takes place. Thus the format

$$\$\ f(i < 0\ |\ \$\ 5d\ \$\ |\ \$\ 10d\ \$)\ \$$$

is equivalent to either of the following, depending on the value of i when transput of some integer takes place:

$$\$\ 5d\ \$$$
$$\$\ 10d\ \$$$

A GENERAL PICTURE contains the letter g and signifies that the value, which may be of any suitable mode, is to appear as it would in formatless transput. For a numeric value and for output only, the g may be followed by a parenthesized list of one, two, or three integer expressions, indicating that the value is to be converted by a call of *whole*, *fixed*, or *float*, respectively. Thus the formatted output on *stand out* of a number *num* according to the picture $g(10,3)$ is equivalent to the effect of the formatless output statement

print (fixed (num, 10, 3))

An integer value can be 'transput' according to a CHOICE PICTURE, which in this case contains the letter c followed by a parenthesized list of one or more string or character denotations (or sequences of them, including replicators) separated by commas. On output, the string in the position given by the integer is written instead of the integer itself; on input, the position number of the string actually read is assigned to the integer name. A Boolean value can similarly be 'transput' according to a choice picture which contains the letter b followed by a parenthesized list of two strings. On output, the first string will be written if the value is **true** and the second string otherwise; on input, the Boolean name will be assigned **true** or **false** depending on which string is read. Examples of choice pictures are given in the following section.

7.3.2 Procedures for Formatted Transput

The principal procedures for formatted transput are *getf* and *putf*. Their use is similar to *get* and *put*, except that the data list may include items of mode **format** but none of mode **proc(ref file)void**. A format item causes the

format to be associated with the file. Any other value is transput according
to the next unused picture in the associated format or, if this contains only
insertions, according to the picture following it. For formatted input
using *stand in*, the following forms are equivalent:

> *readf* (data-list)
> *getf* (*stand in*, data-list)

For formatted output using *stand out*, the following forms are equivalent:

> *print* (data-list)
> *writef* (data-list)
> *putf* (*stand out*, data-list)

As an illustration of formatted output, suppose that the following sequence
has been elaborated:

> **format** *fmt* = $ *l* "ab" x 3z − d, 2(2x 2d.2d) $;
> **int** *i, j*; **real** *x, y, z*;
> **struct** (**int** *a*, **real** *b*) *st*

Then the statement

> *printf* ((*fmt*, 5000, 4.21, 17.3))

gives rise to the output line

> ab   5000   04.21   17.30

Since the printed line must be in complete accord with the format, each
value in the data list must be coerceable to the mode required by the corresponding picture. Thus

> *printf* ((*fmt*, 5000.0, 4.21, 17.3))

is erroneous, but

> *printf* ((*fmt*, 5000, 10, 17.3))

is valid and gives rise to

> ab   5000   10.00   17.30

The statement

  printf((fmt, st, y))

is an example where straightening will be involved.

  On input, the data must be laid out exactly as specified by the format, so that none of the following input lines satisfies *fmt*:

```
ab - 349   12.34   06.70
ab -349    12.34 06.70
ab -349    31564   +6.70
```

On the other hand, since an *x* insertion simply specifies that a character is to be ignored, both of the following are acceptable:

```
ab -349   12.34   06.70
ab* -349**12.34**06.70
```

The statement

  readf ((fmt, i, x, y))

will then result in *i*, *x*, and *y* referring to the values −349, 12.34, and 6.7, respectively. In the case of

  readf ((fmt, z, x, y))

the integer −349 would be widened before being assigned to *z*. However, the statement

  readf ((fmt, i, j, y))

is erroneous since the format ensures that the second input value will be real and hence not assignable to an integer name.

  The number of items in a data list may be less than the number of pictures with frames in the format, and the statements

  printf ((fmt, st)); print (y)

have the same effect as

  printf ((fmt, st, y))

Unless the programmer specifies otherwise (see 7.4), the transput procedures start again at the beginning of the format after the last picture has been used. Thus

> *printf* (*fmt*);
> **to** 5 **do** *printf* ((*st*, *y*)) **od**

results in five identical lines, and

> *printf* ((*fmt*, *1111*, *2.2*, *3.3*, *4444*))

gives rise to

```
ab   1111   02.20   03.30
ab   4444
```

Each time a format association is renewed, the first picture is the next one to be used. Thus

> *printf* ((*fmt*, *1111*, *22*, *fmt*, *33*))

gives rise to

```
ab   1111   22.00
ab     33
```

and not

```
  ab   1111   22.00   33.00
```

A replicator is evaluated only when the picture in which it occurs or the collection which it replicates is needed for control of the next transput operation. If *a* is the flexible name of an integer multiple, for example, the following sequence prints a heading followed by all the elements in its value:

> **file** *stout* := *stand out*;
> *putf* (*stout*, ($ *"values:"* *n*(**upb** *a*) (*2x* +*4d*) $, *a*))

It is necessary to make a local copy of the file because the format text contains an identifier (*a*) with a smaller scope than *stand out*. This situation can arise whenever a format contains a format picture, a general picture, or a replicator consisting of *n* followed by an enclosed clause.

As examples of the use of choice pictures, if *month* currently refers to *3*, the statement

> *printf* (($ *l c("jan", "feb", "march", "april"*),
>   *q 2z* $, *month, 15*))

results in the output

```
march 15
```

Given this as input, the statement

> *read* (($ *c("jan", "feb", "march", "april"*), *q 2z* $, *month, date*))

assigns *3* to *month* and *15* to *date*. If the current value of *flag* is **true**, the statement

> *printf* (($ *l "application ‿" b("accept", "reject") "ed"* $ *flag*))

prints

```
application accepted
```

7.3.3 Non-numeric Facilities (SCO)

For the formatted transput of character and **bytes** data, a format text may contain CHARACTER FRAMES represented by the letter *a*. Character frames can be replicated, and several of them may appear in one picture as long as there are no frames of other types as well. Each character frame controls the transput of exactly one character; when a string of unknown length is to be transput, a general picture is useful. As an example, if *s1* refers to *"abcdef"*, then

> *printf* (($ *l "string ‿ is ‿" " " g " " " "* $, *s1*))

gives rise to the output

```
string is "abcdef"
```

while

> *printf* ($ *l "string ‿ is ‿" l 4a l 2a* $, *s1*))

results in

```
string is
abcd
ef
```

A character frame can be suppressed (*sa*); on input, the effect is as if a blank had been read.

When a string is input according to a *g* picture or using one of the format-less procedures, the default action is to read the remaining characters in the current line. This can be altered by calling the procedure *make term*, of mode **proc(ref file,string)void**, for the relevant file variable:

make term (stand in, "*/")

Now an input string will extend to the first * or / in the data or to the end of the current line, whichever comes first. The terminating character does not form part of the string and should be explicitly spaced over if it is not intended to be the first character of the next input value. When a file *f* is opened,

make term (f, " ")

is in effect elaborated, so that only the end of a line will act as a terminator. (By using a procedure *on line end*, which is described in the next section, it is also possible to prevent the end of a line from terminating a string.)

To illustrate the use of some of these facilities, suppose that we have a large number of cards containing information about the members of an association. To reduce the cost of data preparation, the information for each person has been condensed on a card as follows:

Columns	Data
1 to 5	Membership number
6	Sex (T for male, F for female)
7	Initial
8 to n	Surname ($n > 8$)
$n + 1$ to $n + 2$	Day (01 to 31) ⎫
$n + 3$ to $n + 4$	Month (01 to 12) ⎬ Renewal date
$n + 5$ to $n + 6$	Year (00 to 99) ⎭
$n + 7$ to $n + 11$	Membership fee, without decimal point

Two such input lines might appear as follows:

```
01593Tjsmith15018501812
32811Fmjackson05118600659
```

The number *m* of members is given on a separate card at the beginning. We require a program to print the information in a readable format, each page containing fifty lines with appropriate headings at the top.

It is clearly necessary to use formatted input, with a general picture for the surname. The string will always be terminated by the first digit of the date, i.e., one of the characters *0, 1, 2,* and *3.* The output format in the program below contains a variety of frames and insertions and both types of choice picture. The constant *full pages* represents the number of complete pages in the printout, and *odd lines* the number of lines left over for the last page. For brevity and clarity, a constant for the page heading and a structure variable for the information about a member have been declared.

```
begin
    struct (int no, bool sex, char initial, string surname,
        struct (int day, month, year) date, real fee)
    member;
    string heading = "number" + 5 *blank + "name" + 12 * blank
        + "date" + 8 * blank + "fee";
    make term (stand in, "0123");
    readf ($ 5d, b, a, g, 3(2d), 3ds.2d l $);
    printf ($ l 5d 3q, "m" b("r","s") q, a q, g 25k, 2z q,
        c("jan","feb","mar","apr","may","jun","jul",
        "aug","sep","oct","nov","dec") q,"19" 2d 2q,
        3z.2d $);
    int m; read ((m, newline));
    int full pages = m ÷ 50, odd lines = m mod 50;
    to full pages do
        print ((newpage, heading, newline));
        to 50 do readf (member); printf (member) od
    od;
    if odd lines > 0 then
        print ((newpage, heading, newline));
        to odd lines do readf (member); printf (member) od
    fi
end
```

The information on the two sample cards would be printed at the top of a page as follows:

```
number      name            date        fee

01593   mr j smith      15 jan 1985   18.12
32811   ms m jackson     5 nov 1986    6.59
```

For formatted transput of **bits** values, a picture similar to one for an integer but containing a RADIX FRAME as its first frame may be used. A radix frame consists of the denotation *2, 4, 8,* or *16* followed by the letter *r* and signifies that the value is expressed in binary, quaternary, octal, or hexadecimal notation, respectively. Thus the picture *8r3zd* is consistent with the external representations 7777, 102, and   0.

7.4 Auxiliary Controls for Transput

Several additional predefined procedures are available to help the programmer make allowance for various errors and special circumstances which may arise during transput. Their identifiers and modes are as follows:

page number *line number* *char number* ⎬	**proc(ref file)int**
chan	**proc(ref file)channel**
on logical file end *on physical file end* *on page end* *on line end* *on format end* *on value error*	**proc(ref file,** **proc(ref file)bool)void**
on char error	**proc(ref file,** **proc(ref file,ref char)bool)void**

The first three deliver the components of the current position in the book referred to by a given open file. The procedure *chan* delivers the channel on which the file is open, so that, for example, *chan (stand in)* yields the same value as *stand in channel*.

The procedures beginning with *on* are used to associate new EVENT ROUTINES, mostly of mode **proc(ref file)bool**, with particular open files. Event routines are called automatically by the transput procedures whenever certain situations arise as described below. When an event routine delivers **false**, the transput procedure which called it takes some default action which in some cases depends on the implementation. If it delivers **true**, an attempt is made to continue the transput operation on the assumption that the routine has taken some appropriate remedial action. When a file is opened, all its event routines deliver **false**.

The event routine corresponding to *on logical file end* for the relevant file is called when an input operation or a layout routine has caused the logical end of the book to be reached and further input is attempted; the default action will probably include printing an error message and terminating the program. When the current page number is greater than the number of pages in a book and further transput is attempted, the event routine corresponding to *on physical file end* is called. Similarly, when the current line number (character number) is greater than the number of lines (characters) in the current page (line) and further transput is attempted, the event routine corresponding to *on page end* (*on line end*) is called; the default action is to call *newpage* (*newline*) for the relevant file, except when a string value is being input. The following call specifies that the pages of the printed output of a program are to be numbered at the top:

> *on page end* (*stand out*, (**ref file** f) **bool** : (
>   *newpage* (f);
>   *put* (f, (*"page _ "*, *whole* (*page number* (f)), 0));
>   *newline* (f);
>   **true**))

The event routine corresponding to *on format end* is called when a format is used up before all the values in a data list have been transput. The default action is to go back to the beginning of the format. Alternatively, a programmer-defined event routine may provide a new format and deliver **true**:

> *on format end* (*stand in*, (**ref file** f) **bool** :
>   **if** *char number* (f) $\leq$ *50*
>   **then false**
>   **else** *getf* (f, \$ *l* 10(3d 3x) \$); **true**
>   **fi**)

The event routine corresponding to *on value error* is called when an input value is incompatible with a picture or the number of frames is insufficient. If **true** is delivered, the current value and picture are skipped and transput continues. This routine is also called by any input procedure when the input value cannot be converted to the required mode, such as when an integer is larger than *max int*.

The event routine corresponding to *on char error* is called during formatted input when an incoming character does not match the relevant frame. In each case, a reference to a suggested replacement character is supplied as an actual parameter. The character 0 is suggested for a digit or zero frame, $+$ for a sign frame, . for a point frame, $_{10}$ for an exponent frame, $\perp$ for a complex frame, and *flop* for a Boolean frame. Situations where $0, \perp$, or *flop* is suggested may also arise during formatless input. The default action will probably include printing an error message. If the event routine delivers **true**, however, the erroneous character is replaced by the suggested one, which the routine may have changed, and the input operation is continued.

Each channel has an associated CONVERSION KEY which specifies the correspondence between the internal and external representations of characters for that channel. The call *stand conv* (*c*) yields the conversion key for a channel *c*, and there may be environment enquiries for other keys. When a file *f* is opened on *c*, *stand conv* (*c*) is associated with *f*. This association may then be changed by calling the predefined procedure *make conv*:

> *make conv* (*f*, *stand conv* (*stand out channel*))

7.5 Binary Transput

In both formatless and formatted transput, the external data is in a well-defined character form which, when represented on paper, is readable by humans. A third form of transput, called BINARY transput, can be used when the data is to be produced and used only by a program or programs. In such cases binary transput is likely to be more efficient than the other forms.

The main predefined procedures for binary output and input are *put bin* and *get bin*, respectively. In each case, the first parameter specifies an open file *f* where *bin possible* (*f*) would yield **true**; the second parameter is a data list as for *read* or *print*, except that **proc(ref file)void** items are not permitted. The data list in a call of *put bin* is straightened as before and output in a form which is unspecified except that the data may be re-input by a call of *get bin* where each mode in the straightened list of names is a reference to the mode of the corresponding value that was output. Binary transput operations advance the current position in the book in the normal way; as default actions, *newline* and *newpage* are called automatically when necessary.

To illustrate these points, suppose that a file *f* has been suitably opened and that the following declarations are in effect:

> [*10*] **int** *z*;
> **real** *x*;
> **struct** (**real** *a*, **int** *b*) *y*

Then the following statements will output in binary form a real number, ten integers, another real, and another integer in that order:

> *reset* (*f*);
> *put bin* (*f*, (*x*, *z*, *y*))

Some time later, these values can be restored exactly as they were by

> *reset* (*f*);

get bin (f, (x, z, y))

The following statements would be valid also, but the values of the various variables would be rearranged:

reset (f);
get bin (f, (y, $z[:9]$, x, $z[10]$))

When the standard backup file is used, the following forms are equivalent:

write bin (data-list)
put bin (*stand back*, data-list)

The following forms are also equivalent:

read bin (data-list)
get bin (*stand back*, data-list)

Binary and non-binary data are completely incompatible as far as the transput procedures are concerned. Unless the book permits random access, the file must be reset before switching from one type of transput to the other.

Chapter 8

Additional Control Devices

8.1 Labels, Jumps, and Completers

A unit can sometimes be preceded by a LABEL, which consists of an identifier followed by a colon. A labelled unit is itself a unit, so that a statement or expression may be preceded by more than one label. The scope of a label identifier is confined to the range in which it occurs, and the nesting rules are the same as for other identifiers. A unit can be labelled only if it comes after all the declarations in the series in which it occurs. Thus the sequence

> **int** i; *input* : *read* (i); **int** j

is incorrect, whereas the following is valid:

> **int** i;
> (**int** j; *input* : *read* ((i, j)); ...);
> **int** k

The units in the series following an **if**, **elif**, **case**, **ouse**, or **while** symbol cannot be labelled. The identifier *stop* is an implicitly defined label identifier which can be thought of as occurring just past the end of any program.

The presence of a label does not affect the elaboration of the unit following it. Its purpose is rather to mark the unit as the destination of one or more JUMPS situated somewhere within the scope of the label identifier. A jump is a statement consisting of a label identifier, optionally preceded by the symbol **goto** or by the two symbols **go to**. Thus the following jumps are equivalent:

> *input*
> **goto** *input*
> **go to** *input*

The effect of elaborating a jump is to modify the normal sequential elaboration of phrases in such a way that the phrase elaborated immediately after the jump is the unit with the corresponding label; thereafter, elaboration continues from the latter point in the program in the usual way. In the case of a jump from within a routine to some point in an enclosing range, elaboration of the phrase which invoked the routine is abandoned.

For reasons of correctness and clarity of programs, it is good practice to use labels and jumps only as a last resort when all other constructs, such as loop clauses, conditional clauses, and procedures, either are inapplicable or give rise to appreciable inefficiency or inconvenience. Thus, although it would be possible in principle to write a program for any task using only jumps and a rudimentary form of conditional clause to control the sequence of elaboration, we only mention some of the few situations where this type of programming is advantageous.

Several examples involving the label identifier *stop* have been given already; programmer-defined labels could equally well be used in these situations. Another use of jumps is in writing event routines, especially ones corresponding to *on logical file end*, when the transput operation is to be abandoned altogether and another part of the program begun. In the following sequence, all the data values are input and their sum formed before beginning the part of the program starting at the label identifier *proceed*:

```
int a, s := 0;
file stin := stand in;
on logical file end (stin, (ref file f) bool : proceed);
do get (stin, a); s plusab a od;
proceed: . . .
```

When the end of the data is reached, the jump will terminate the event routine, the transput procedure (*get*) which called it, and the loop containing the call of the transput procedure. It is necessary to make a local copy of the file because the scope of the identifier *proceed* is smaller than that of *stand in*.

A COMPLETER consists of the symbol **exit** followed by a label and may appear between two units wherever a semicolon followed by a label would also be valid. When a completer is elaborated, the innermost series in which it occurs is terminated and yields as its value the value of the unit preceding the completer. As an example, the following procedure tests an integer for membership in a multiple:

```
proc member =  (ref [ ] int a, int b) bool : (
    for i from lwb a to upb a do
        if b = a[i] then t fi
    od;
    false exit
```

t : **true**)

In the following alternative version, the use of jumps is avoided:

proc *member* = (**ref** [ ] **int** *a*, **int** *b*) **bool** : (
    bool *not found*;
    for *i* **from lwb** *a* **to upb** *a*
    while *not found* := $b \neq a[i]$
    do skip od;
    not *not found*)

A series which yields a value can contain any number of completers. Together with the final expression, the units preceding them may be balanced in the same way as the constituents of a case clause.

8.2 Collateral Elaboration

In COLLATERAL, as opposed to serial, elaboration, there is no definite sequential order in which a set of actions is carried out. Roughly speaking, the constituents of any construct which are at the same scope level and which are not separated by semicolons are elaborated collaterally.This includes all of the following sets of constituents:

the two sides of an assignation
parts of a declaration separated by commas
operands of a dyadic formula
subscripts or trimmers in a slice
actual parameters in a call
items in a data list in a transput statement
the **from**, **to**, and **by** parts of a loop clause
elements of a row or structure display

Collaterality implies that the result of elaborating these constructs is in some cases unpredictable. As a simple example, we should avoid writing the formula

$$(i := 5) + i$$

since, if the previous value of i is different from 5, the resulting value depends on the order in which the operands are elaborated.

A COLLATERAL CLAUSE is a list of two or more units separated by commas and enclosed by (and) or **begin** and **end**. Row displays and structure displays are both collateral expressions; in a COLLATERAL STATEMENT, on the other hand, each unit is a statement:

$(i := 1, j := 2, print\ (k)\ )$

A PARALLEL CLAUSE is similar to a collateral statement except that it is preceded by the symbol **par**. A parallel clause is used when the constituent statements, which in this context are said to specify PROCESSES, are to be actually elaborated simultaneously. Then if each process does a substantial amount of work and includes some actions which affect other processes, it becomes necessary to SYNCHRONIZE them, i.e., to exert some control over their relative progress. To provide this control, we have the special mode **sema** (for 'semaphore'), each value of which includes a **ref int**, and the following monadic operators: **level** yields a semaphore referring to the value of its integer operand or the integer referred to by its semaphore operand; **down**, applied to a semaphore referring to an integer i, suspends the elaboration of the statement in which it occurs if i is zero and decreases i by one otherwise; **up**, applied to a semaphore referring to an integer i, increases i by 1, and all statements previously suspended by the same semaphore are resumed. The synchronization operators **down** and **up** are useful only in parallel clauses. They are the only predefined operators in the language which do not deliver values:

Symbols	Priority	Modes
down	*10*	(**sema**) **void**
up	*10*	(**sema**) **void**
level	*10*	(**int**) **sema**
		(**sema**) **int**

A description of parallel processing techniques and their use in realistic examples is beyond the scope of this book. The program given below simply inputs and outputs an indefinitely long sequence of integer values with at most *100* values stored in the main memory before being printed:

```
begin
    [100] int buffer;
    int inp := 0, outp := 0;
    sema used := level 0, unused := level 100;
    par (do down unused;
        inp modab 100 plusab 1;
        read (buffer[inp]);
        up used
    od,
    do down used;
        outp modab 100 plusab 1;
```

```
            print (buffer[outp]);
            up unused
        od)
    end
```

The variables *inp* and *outp* keep track of the last elements read and printed; the semaphore *used* refers to the number of values read but not yet printed and causes the suspension of the printing process when there are no such values; *unused* refers to the number of buffer elements available for reading and causes the suspension of the reading process when all the elements are values not yet printed. The idea is to make better use of the input and output channels, which may operate at different rates and which are assumed to be directly controlled by the program. In practice, more than one value at a time would be transput.

Answers to Exercises

Section 1.1

1. Divide the number by *2*. If there is no remainder, divide it by the odd numbers *3, 5*, etc., until either there is no remainder or the square root of the number is reached. In the former case the number is not prime and in the latter case it is.
2. Add the first two numbers. Add the third number to this sum to form a new sum. Add the fourth number to this sum and so on until the sum of all *n* numbers is obtained. Divide this by *n* to obtain the average.

Section 1.3.3

1. *143   00   3*
2. *" "* (*0* characters)
   "a1b2c3" (*6* characters)
   " " "ab" "c" (*5* characters)
3. $1_{10}1$ *63.123e − 10*

Section 1.4

1. *b2z   ttt*   real
2. **real** *sum, mean*
   int *number of numbers*

Section 1.5.1.1

1. (a) *5*   (b) *− 15*   (c) *8*
2. (a) *15*   (b) *250*   (c) *2*

Section 1.5.1.3

1. (a) **int**, *2*   (b) **real**, *2.5*
   (c) **real**, *13.0*   (d) **int**, *2*

(e) **int**, *3* (f) **real**, *6.5*
(g) **real**, *0.26* (h) **real**, *6.76*

Section 1.5.2

1. (a) **string**, *"bcde"* (b) **char**, *"*"*
   (c) **int**, *11* (d) **string**, *"abcdeff"*
   (e) **string**, *"cddedede"*

Section 2.1.1

1. (a) *i* is assigned *8*
   (b) *x* is assigned *8.0*
   (c) *i* is assigned *3*
       j is assigned *3*
       y is assigned *3.0*
   (d) *i* is assigned *2*
   (e) *y* is assigned *4.8*
       x is assigned *4.8*
2. (b) Dereferencing *j*. Addition. Widening. Assignment to *x*.
   (c) Dereferencing *x*. Dereferencing *y*. Multiplication. Chopping (**entier**). Assignment to *i*. Dereferencing *i*. Assignment to *j*. Dereferencing *j*. Widening. Assignment to *y*.
   (d) Dereferencing *j*. Addition. Dereferencing *i* (could have been done first). Remainder from integer division. Assignment to *i*.
   (e) Dereferencing *y*. Dereferencing *i*. Multiplication. Assignment to *y*. Dereferencing *y*. Assignment to *x*.
3. (a) Incompatible modes on left and right sides.
   (b) Left side of right assignation does not yield a name.
   (c) Incorrect mixture of operand modes.
   (d) Left operand of **divab** does not yield a name.
   (e) Left operand of **plusab** does not yield a name.
4. (a) *j* **minusab** *1* (b) *x* **timesab** *y*
   (c) *i* **plusab** *i* + *1* (d) *y* **timesab** *x* * *5*
   (e) *x* := *y* **divab** *j*

Section 2.1.2

1. (a) *s1* is assigned *"5pqrst"*
   (b) *s1* is assigned *"a"*
   (c) *c1* is assigned the character corresponding to *24*
       s1 is assigned the string obtained by rowing the above value
   (d) *s2* is changed to *"pqbcd"*

s1 is changed to *"bcdd"*

(e) *s1* is assigned *"5abcd"*

(f) *s2* is assigned *"pqrstpqrs"*

s1 is assigned *"pqrstpqrs"*

2. (a) Incompatible modes.

(b) Incompatible modes.

(c) Right side of incorrect length.

(d) Right side of equivalent explicit assignation yields string of incorrect length.

(e) Right operand does not yield a name.

Section 2.3.1

1. (a) (1) Declaration. (2) Unit. (3) Unit.

(1) Two names of mode **ref int**, represented by *a* and *b*, are created. (2) Two integer values are input for *a* and *b*. (3) The sum, product, and integer quotient of these values are calculated and printed in order.

(b) (1) Declaration. (2) Unit. (3) Declaration. (4) Unit. (5) Unit.

(1) Three names of mode **ref int**, represented by *x*, *y*, and *z*, are created. (2) Three integers are input as their values. (3) A name of mode **ref real**, represented by *avg*, is created. (4) The average (**real**) of the three values is calculated and assigned to *avg*. The name yielded by the phrase is voided. (5) The average and the absolute differences between the average and the three values are printed.

2. (a) Variable declared twice.

(b) Variable used before it is declared.

(c) Last phrase is a declaration.

(d) Meaningless symbols *"--"* appear outside a comment.

(e) Use of an undeclared identifier.

Section 2.3.2

1. (**int** *a, b, c, d, e*;
   read ((a, b, c, d, e));
   print (($a + b + c + d + e$) / 5))

2. (**int** *i, j, isq, jsq*; *read* ((i, j));
   isq := $i * i$; *jsq* := $j * j$;
   print (($isq, jsq, isq + jsq, isq - jsq$)))

Section 2.3.4

1. (**string** *s4* = *"****"*;

string *s8* = *s4* + *s4*; **string** *s12* = *s8* + *s4*;
print ((*s4*, *newline*, *s8*, *newline*, *s12*, *newline*,
    s8, *newline*, *s4*)))

2. (a) (**string** *line1*, *line2*;
    read ((*line1*, *newline*, *line2*));
    print ((*line1*[*1*:*40*], *newline*, *line1*[*41*:*80*],
        newline, *line2*[*1*:*40*], *newline*, *line2*[*41*:*80*])))

  (b) (**string** *line*; *read* (*line*);
    print ((*line*[*1*:*40*], *newline*, *line* [*41*:*80*]));
    read ((*newline*, *line*));
    print ((*newline*, *line*[*1*:*40*], *newline*, *line*[*41*:*80*])))

3. (**string** *s4* = *"****"*; **string** *stars* := *s4*;
  print (*stars*);
  print ((*newline*, *stars* **plusab** *s4*));
  print ((*newline*, *stars* + *s4*)))

Section 2.3.5

1. (**real** *a*, *b*, *c*; *read* ((*a*, *b*, *c*));
  real *s* = (*a* + *b* + *c*) / *2*;
  print (*sqrt* (*s* * (*s* − *a*) * (*s* − *b*) * *s* − *c*))))

2. (**real** *a*, *b*, *c*; *read* ((*a*, *b*, *c*));
  real *s* := (*a* + *b* + *c*) / *2*;
  print (*sqrt* (*s* * (*s* − *a*) * (*s* − *b*)* (*s* − *c*)));
  read ((*a*, *b*, *c*));
  s := (*a* + *b* + *c*) / *2*;
  print (*sqrt* (*s* * (*s* −*a*) * (*s* − *b*) * (*s* − *c*))))

3. (**real** *twopi* = *2* * *pi*;
  real *s*, *y*; *read* ((*x*, *y*));
  real *sum* := *x* = *y*;
  print (*exp* (*x* − *y*) * *sin* (*sum*) * *cos* (*sum*) *
    ln (*arc cos* (*x*)) / *twopi*);
  read ((*x*, *y*)); *sum* := *x* + *y*;
  print (*exp* (*x* − *y*) * *sin* (*sum*)* *cos* (*sum*) *
    ln (*arc cos* (*x*)) / *twopi*))

Section 3.1

1. (a) No semicolon separating inner closed clause from following state-
    ment; use of *y* outside its range.
  (b) Semicolon after the last phrase in a series.
  (c) Right side of assignation not an expression.

(d) *x* used outside its range.
2. (**int** *y*, *z*; *read* ((*y*, *z*));
    int *x* = 2 * (*y* + *z*);
    print ((*x*, 2 * *x*)))

Section 3.2.1

1. (a) Semicolon following **do**.
  (b) Two attempts to change the value of the constant *i*.
  (c) **from** part must precede **by** part.
2. (a) *10*   (b) *0*   (c) *4*   (d) *11*

Section 3.2.2

1. *f* := *1*; **for** *i* **to** *n* **do** *f* **timesab** *i* **od**
2. (**int** *n*, *f*;
    to *100* **do** *read* (*n*); *f* := *1*;
           for *i* **to** *n* **do** *f* **timesab** *i* **od**;
           print (*f*)
      od)

Section 3.2.3

1. (**string** *str*; *read* (*str*);
    int *len* = **upb** *str*;
    for *i* **to** *len* **do** *print* ((*str*[*i* :*len*], *newline*)) **od**)
2. (**string** *in*, *out* := " "; *read* (*in*);
    for *i* **to** **upb** *in* **do** *out* **plusab** *in*[*i*] + *blank* **od**;
    to *50* **do** *print* ((*out*, *newline*)) **od**)

Section 3.2.4

1. (**real** *p* := *0*, *q* := *0*, *r* := *0*, *s* := *0*, *x*, *y*;
    int *n*; *read* (*n*);
    to *n* **do** *read* ((*x*, *y*));
           p **plusab** *x*; *q* **plusab** *y*;
           r **plusab** *x* * *x*; *s* **plusab** *x* * *y*
      od;
    real *b* = (*q* * *p* − *n* * *s*) / (*p* * *p* − *n* * *r*);
    real *a* = (*s* − *b* * *r*) / *p*;
    print ((*a*, *b*)))

Section 3.3.2

1. ([*20*] **int** *a*; **int** *sum* := *0*;

```
    for i to 20 do read (a[i]); sum plusab a[i] od;
  - real avg  =  sum / 20;
    for i to 20 do print (a[i] −avg) od )
2. ( int n; read (n); [0:n] int a, b;
    for i from 0 to n do read ((a[i], b[i])) od;
    for i from n by −1 to 0 do
      print ((a[i] + b[i], a[i] −b[i], newline))
    od )
3. ( 5, 5] int power; int sum;
    for a to 5 do
      for b to 5 do power[a,b] := a ↑ b od
    od;
    for a to 5 do sum := 0;
                  for b to 5 do sum plusab power[a, b] od;
                  print (sum)
    od;
    print (newline);
    for b to 5 do sum := 0;
                  for a to 5 do sum plusab power[a,b] od;
                  print (sum)
    od )
```

Section 3.3.3

```
1. ( [10] int a, b; read ((a, b));
    print ((a, newline, b, newline));
    for i to 10 do print (a[i] + b[i]) od;
    print (newline);
    for i to 10 do print (a[i] −b[i]) od )
2. ( [ ] int pr1  =  (2, 3, 5, 7, 11, 17, 19, 23, 29);
    [10] int pr2;
    for i to 10 do pr2[i] := pr1[11 − i] od;
    to 25 do print (( pr1, newline, pr2, newline)) od )
```

Section 3.3.4

```
1. ( [10, 10] int table; read (table);
    for j to 10 do print ((table [,j], newline)) od )
2. ( [50] int fifty; read (fifty);
    [10] int ten; int sum;
    for i to 41 do
      ten := fifty [i : i + 9];
      sum := 0;
```

```
    for j to 10 do sum plusab ten[j] od;
    print ((ten, sum, newline))
od )
```

Section 3.3.7

1. (**int** *n*; *read* ((*n*, *newline*));
   [*n*] **char** *in*; *read* (*in*);
   for *i* **to** *n* **do** *print* ((*120* ∗ *in*[*i*], *newline*)) **od**)
2. ([*50, 70*] **char** *page*; [ ] **char** *b10* = *blank* ∗ *10*;
   for *i* **to** *50* **do** *page*[*i*, *31:40*] := *b10* **od**;
   int *n*; *read* ((*n*, *newline*));
   to *n* ÷ *100* **do**
      print (*newpage*);
      for *i* **to** *50* **do** *read* ((*page*[*i*, : *30*], *newline*)) **od**;
      for *i* **to** *50* **do** *read* ((*page*[*i*, *41* :], *newline*)) **od**;
      for *i* **to** *50* **do** *print* ((*page*[*i*,], *newline*)) **od**
   od)

Section 3.3.8

1. *minor*[:3, :4] := *x*[:3, :4];
   minor[:3, 5:] := *x*[:3, 6:];
   minor[4:, :4] := *x*[5:, :4];
   minor[4:, 5:] := *x*[5:, 6:]
2. (**int** *m*, *n*, *p*; *read* ((*m*, *n*, *p*));
   [*m*:*n*] **real** *a*; [*n*:*p*] **real** *b*; *read* ((*a*, *b*));
   [*m*:*p*] **real** *c*, *c2*, *c2m1*;
   for *i* **to** *m* **do**
      ref [ ] **real** *arow* = *a*[*i*,];
      for *j* **to** *p* **do**
         ref [ ] **real** *bcol* = *b*[,*j*];
         ref real *cij* = *c*[*i*,*j*] := *0*;
         for *k* **to** *n* **do** *cij* **plusab** *arow*[*k*] ∗ *bcol*[*k*] **od**;
         c2m1 [*i*, *j*] := (*c2*[*i*, *j*] := *2* ∗ *cij*) − *1*
      od
   od;
   for *i* **to** *m* **do**
      print ((*c*[*i*,], *space*, *c2*[*i*,], *space*, *c2m1*[*i*,], *newline*))
   od)

Section 4.2

1. (a) **true**   (b) **true**   (c) *7*

2. (a) $<$ not defined for a Boolean operand.
   (b) **or** not defined for an integer operand.
   (c) $\geq$ not defined for a Boolean operand.

Section 4.3.1

2. (a) $(i = 0 \textbf{ or } j = 0 \mid x := y; y \textbf{ plusab } z)$
   (b) $(\textbf{odd } i \mid i \textbf{ plusab } 1 \mid i \textbf{ minusab } 1)$
   (c) $(b1 \mid 5 \mid \textbf{int } k; read(k); k)$
   (d) $\textbf{upb } (b1 \mid a := (1, 2, 3, 4, 5) \mid b := ( ))$
   (e) $((b1 \mid b2 \mid \textbf{false}) \mid print(x))$
3. (**int** i, j, k; $read((i, j, k))$;
   $print$ (**if** $i < j$ **and** $j < k$ **then** "yes" **else** "no" **fi**))

Section 4.3.2

1. **if** a **then** b **elif** c **then if** d **then** e **fi else** f **fi**
   $(a \mid b \mid : c \mid (d \mid e) \mid f)$
2. **if** a **then if** b **then** c **else if** d **then** e **else if** f
         then g **fi fi fi fi**
3. $(n + 3 \mid a, b, c, d \mid e)$

Section 4.4.1

1. **bool** *not found* := **true**;
   for i **to** m **while** *not found* **do**
      ref [ ] **int** *row* $= aa[i,]$;
      for j **to** n **while** *not found* **do**
        if $row[j] = p$ **then** *not found* := : **false**
        else $print(row[j])$ **fi**
      od
   od
2. **for** i **to** m **do**
      ref [ ] **int** *row* $= aa[i,]$;
      for j **to** n **do**
        if $row[j] = p$ **then** *stop* **fi**;
        $print(row[j])$
      od
   od
3. (**int** $x, n := 0, s := 0$; $read(x)$;
   while $x \neq 0$ **do** n **plusab** 1; s **plusab** x; $read(x)$ **od**;
   $print$ (**if** $n = 0$ **then** 0 **else** s / n **fi**))

Section 4.4.2

```
1. ( string s; char stopper = "←";
     read ((s, newline));
     while s[1] ≠ stopper do
        for i to upb s do (s[i] ≠ blank | print (s[i])) od;
        print (newline);
        read ((s, newline))
     od )
2. ( string s, t; char stopper = "←";
     string b60 = blank * 60;
     read ((s, newline));
     while s[1] ≠ stopper do
        t := " ";
        for i to upb s do (s[i] ≠ blank   t plusab s[i]) od;
        print ((b60[ :60 − upb t ÷ 2], t, newline));
        read ( (s, newline) )
     od )
```

Section 4.4.3

```
1. real arc tanh := 0, term := x;
   for i from 3 by 2 while term > small real do
     arc tanh plusab term; term := x ↑ i / i
   od
2. ( real xold := 0, xnew := 0.5;
     while abs (xnew − xold) > small real do
        xold := xnew; xnew := cos (xold) od;
     print (xnew) )
3. ( int n; read (n); real t;
     [n,n] real a; [n] real b, x;
     for i to n do
        read ((a[i,], b[i])); x[i] := 0 od;
     bool active := true;
     while active do
        active := false;
        for i to n do
           ref [ ] real arow = a[i,];
           t := b[i];
           for j to i − 1 do t minusab arow [j] * x[j] od;
           for j from i + 1 to n do t minusab arow [j] * x [j] od;
           t divab arow[i];
           if abs (t − x[i]) > small real then active := true fi;
```

$$x[i] := t$$
od
od;
print (x))

Section 5.2.1

1. (a) **proc** *sg* = **int** : $x + y$
   (b) **proc** *si* = **int** : (**int** x, y; *read* $((x, y))$; $x + y$)
2. (**proc** *io* = **void** :
      (**int** x; **to** *10* **do** *read* (x); *print* (x) **od**);
   io; *io*; *io*)
3. (a) **proc** *mn* = **ref** [ ] **int** : (
         int n; *read* (n);
         heap [n] **int** m; *read* (m);
         m)
   (b) **ref** [ ] **int** v = *mn*

Section 5.2.2

1. (a) (**int** $a = w, b = x, c = y$, **ref int** $d = z$;
         $d := (a \mid a + b, a - b, a * b \mid 0)$)
   (b) (**int** $a = i := j, b = e$ **plusab** $f, c = 5$, **ref int** $d = k$;
         $d := (a \mid a + b, a - b, a * b \mid 0)$)
2. **proc** *arith* = (**int** a, b, **ref int** c, d, e, f) **void** :
      $(c := a + b; d := a - b; e := a * b; f := a \div b)$;
   arith $(20, 30, i, j, k, l)$
3. **proc** *sub* = (**ref** [ ] **int** a, **int** b) [ ] **int** : (
   int m = **lwb** a, n = **upb** a; [$m:n$] **int** c;
   for i **from** m **to** n **do** $c[i] := a[i] - b$ **od**;
   c)
4. **proc** *compare* = (**ref** [ ] **int** a, b [ ] **bool** :
   if int n = **upb** a; **lwb** $a = 1$ **and lwb** $b = 1$ **and upb** $b = n$
   then [n] **bool** c;
      for i **to** n **do** $c[i] := a[i] > b[i]$ **od**;
      c
   fi

Section 5.2.3

1. (a) **proc** p = (**bool** f)**proc**(int,int)int :
         if f
         then (**int** a, b) **int** : $a * a + b * b$

    else (**int** a, b) **int** : $a * a - b * b$
    fi
 (b) p (**true**) $(4, 5)$
2. **proc** ncr = (**int** n, r) **int** :
  $(r = 1 \mid n \mid ncr (n, r - 1) * (n - r + 1) \div r)$

Section 5.3

1. **prio vs** = 6;
 op vs = (**ref int** a, b) **int** : $a + b$
2. **op** + = ([ ] **int** a, b) [ ] **int** : (
    [10] **int** c;
    for i **to** 10 **do** $c[i] := a[$**at** $1] [i] + b[$**at** $1] [i]$ **od**; c),
  + = ([ ] **real** a, b) [ ] **real** : (
    [10] **real** c;
    for i **to** 10 **do** $c[i] := a$ [**at** $1][i] + b[$**at** $1] [i]$ **od**; c),
  + = ([ ] **int** a, [ ] **real** b) [ ] **real** : (
    [10] **real** c;
    for i **to** 10 **do** $c[i] := a[$**at** $1] [i] + b[$**at**$1] [i]$ **od**; c),
  + = ([ ] **real** a, [ ] **int** b) [ ] **real** : (
    [10] **real** c;
    for i **to** 10 **do** $c[i] := a[$**at** $1] [i] + b[$**at** $1] [i]$ **od**; c)

Section 5.4

1. **op sb** = (**string** s) **string** : (
  int $i := $ **lwb** s;
  from i **to upb** s **while** $s[i] = blank$ **do** i **plusab** 1 **od**;
  $s[i:]$)
2. **int** $i := $ **lwb** s, j; **int** $k := i - 2$;
 bool $b := char\ in\ string\ (blank, j, s)$;
 while b **do**
  k **plusab** j;
  if $i \leq k$ **then** $print\ ((s[i:k], newline))$ **fi**;
  $b := char\ in\ string\ (blank, j, s[i := k + 2 :])$ **od**;
 $print\ (s[i:])$
3. **proc** $append$ = (**ref flex** [ ] **string** rs, **string** s) **void** : (
  int n = **upb** rs; [$n + 1$] **string** t;
  $t[1:n] := rs$;
  $t[n + 1] := s$;
  $rs := t$)
4. **proc** $search$ = (**ref** [ ] **string** rs, **string** s) **int** : (
  int $m1 := 0, m2 := $ **upb** $rs + 1, psn := 0, i$;

```
  while psn = 0 and m2 − m1 > 1 do
    ref string rsi = rs[i := (m1 + m2) ÷ 2];
    (rsi = s | psn | :rsi > s | m2 | m1) := i od;
  psn )
```

Section 5.5

1. **op mean** = **(ref [] real** a**) real** : (
   real $s := 0$;
   for i **from lwb** a **to upb** a **do** s **plusab** $a[i]$ **od**;
   s / **upb** a[**at** 1] ¢ assuming a is not empty ¢)
2. **proc** nr = **(proc(real) real** f, g, **real** $init$**) real** : (
   real $xnew := init$; **real** $xold := xnew + 1$;
   while abs $(xnew − xold) >$ **small real do**
     $xold := xnew$;
     $xnew := xold − f(xold) / g(xold)$ **od**;
   $xnew$)
3. **op** + = **(ref [ ] flex [ ] real** a, b**) ref [ ] flex [ ] real** :
   if int n = **upb** a; **lwb** a = 1 **and lwb** b = 1 **and upb** b = n
   then heap $[n]$ **flex [ ] real** c;
     for i **to** n **do**
       $[i]$ **real** row; **ref [ ] real** ai = $a[i], bi$ = $b[i]$;
       for j **to** i **do** $row[j] := ai[j] + bi[j]$ **od**;
       $c[i] := row$
     od;
     c
   fi

Section 6.2.1

1. **mode rri** = **ref ref int**,
        rrr = **ref ref real**,
        rrb = **ref ref bool**,
        rrri = **ref ref ref int**
2. (a) none
   (b) dereferencing ip and i
   (c) dereferencing i, ip twice
   (d) none
3. (a) Left side cannot be dereferenced.
   (b) Left side must yield a name.
   (c) **ref ref int** cannot be coerced to **ref real**.

Section 6.3.1

1. (a) **mode rtl** = **struct (int** num, den**)**

(b) **struct** (**real** *x*, **int** *y*) *s*

(c) **mode bitstr** = **struct** ([*20*] **bool** *b*),

      rr = **struct** (**flex** [*1* :*0*] **real** *a*, **int** *b*)

2. (a) The mode of a field cannot be the mode of the structure itself.

  (b) Two fields of the same mode cannot have the same selector.

  (c) The modes **ref struct** (**int** *a*, *b*) and

     ref struct (**int** *a*, *c*) are incompatible.

  (d) (*a* **of** *b*) is not a selector.

3. (a) *a* **of** *b* **of** *c*   (b) *a* **of** *b*[*i*]

  (c) *a* **of** *b* (*c*)   (d) no change

Section 6.3.2

1. **mode book** = **struct** (**string** *author*, *title*, *publisher*,

                int *year*, **struct** (**int** *day*, *month*, *year*)

                date, **real** *price*, *class*)

2. **proc** *books in year* = (**ref** [] **book** *lib*, **int** *y*) [] **int** : (

  int *n* = **upb** *lib*; [*n*] **int** *biy*; **int** *j* := *0*;

  for *i* **to** *n* **do**

    if *year* **of** *lib*[*i*] = *y* **then** *biy*[*j* **plusab** *1*] := *i* **fi**

  od ;

  biy[:*j*])

Section 6.3.3

1. **op** ↑ = (**rtl** *a*, **int** *b*) **rtl** : (*num* **of** *r* ↑ *b*) **r** (*den* **of** *r* ↑ *b*)

2. **mode quad** = **struct** (**rtl** *c2*, *c1*, *c0*);

  proc *prod* = (**quad** *a*, *b*) **quad** :

    c2 **of** *a* ∗ *c0* **of** *b* + *c1* **of** *a* ∗ *c1* **of** *b*

        + *c0* **of** *a* ∗ *c0* **of** *b*,

    c1 **of** *a* ∗ *c0* **of** *b* + *c0* **of** *a* ∗ *c1* **of** *b*,

    c0 **of** *a* ∗ *c0* **of** *b*)

Section 6.4

1. (a) **proc int** can be deprocedured to **int**.

  (b) Bounds must not be included.

  (c) *ir* cannot be 'deunited' to **int**.

  (d) **void** should be parenthesized.

2. **proc** *add* = (**brent** *a*, *b*) **brent** :

  case *a*

  in (**int** *i*) : **case** *b*

       in (*int j*) : *i* + *j*,

```
                        (real y) : i + y
                    out skip
                    esac,
            (real x) : case b
                        in (int j) : x + j,
                           (real y) : x + y
                        out skip
                        esac,
            (bool p): case b
                        in (bool q) : p and q
                        out skip
                        esac
        esac
```

Section 6.5

1. **op** ↓ = ([ ] **char** s, **ref ref node** chn) **void** :
   chn := **heap node** := (s, chn);
   op ↑ = (**ref ref node** chn) [ ] **char** : (
   [ ] **char** s = *info* **of** chn;
   chn := *next* **of** chn;
   s)

2. **proc** *update* = (**ref string** s, **ref ref btnode** r) **void** : (
   ref ref btnode ptr := r; **bool** b := **true**;
   while b **do**
       if ref btnode (ptr) **is nil**
       then ref ref btnode (ptr) := **heap btnode** :=
           (s, 1, **nil**, **nil**); b := **false**
       elif s < *val* **of** ptr
       then ptr := *left* **of** ptr
       elif s > *val* **of** ptr
       then ptr := *right* **of** ptr
       else *num* **of** ptr **plusab** 1; b := **false**
       fi
   od)

3. **proc** *reverse* = (**operand** a) **operand** :
   case a
   in (**char** c) : c,
       (**ref expr** e) : **heap expr** := (*reverse* (*opd2* **of** e),
           opr **of** e, *reverse* (*opd1* **of** e))
   esac

Section 6.6.1

1. **op** + = (**int** a, **long int** b) **long int** : **leng** a + b,

```
      +  =  (long int a, int b) long int : a  +  leng b
2. mode intno  =  union (short int, int, long int);
   proc fact  =  (int a) intno : (
      long int li := long 1;
      for i from 2 to a do li timesab leng i od;
      if li ≤ leng max int
      then if li ≤ leng short max int
         then shorten shorten li else shorten li fi
      else li
      fi )
```

Section 6.6.2

```
1. proc e  =  (real x) real : (
      long real expx := long 0, term := long 1;
      for n while abs term > long small real do
         expx plusab term;
         term timesab x / leng n od;
      shorten expx )
2. mode realno  =  union (real, long real, short real);
   proc nat log  =  (realno x) realno :
      case x
      in (real r) : ln (r),
         (long real lr) : long ln (lr),
         (short real sr) : short ln (sr)
      esac
```

Section 6.6.3

```
1. proc cexp  =  (compl c) compl :
      exp (re c) ∗ cos (im c) i sin im c)
2. proc tab  =  (proc(compl) compl f, ref [ ] compl a) void :
      for i from lwb a to upb a do
         print ((a[i], f(a[i]), newline)) od;
   [25] compl c := ( −2 i −2, −2 i −1, −2 i 0, −2 i 1,
      −2 i 2, −1 i −2, −1 i −1, −1 i 0 −1 i 1, −1 i 2,
      0 i −2, 0 i −1, 0 i 0, 0 i 1, 0 i 2, 1 i −2,
      1 i −1, 1 i 0, 1 i 1, 1 i 2, 2 i −2, 2 i −1,
      2 i 0, 2 i 1, 2 i 2);
   tab (cexp, c)
```

Appendix I
Alternative Symbol Representations

The following table summarizes all the equivalent symbol representations other than predefined operator symbols, which are given in the various operator tables in the text. It should be borne in mind that a particular implementation may not permit all the alternative forms and may permit others not given here.

Context	Alternatives
Real denotation	e $_{10}$ $\backslash$
Character or string denotation	$\dot{-}$ space character
Closed, collateral, or parallel clause	**begin** ... **end** (...)
Conditional clause	**if** ... **then** ... **elif** ... **else** ... **fi** (... | ... |: ... | ...)
Case or conformity clause	**case** ... **in** ... **ouse** ... **out** ... **esac** (... | ... |: ... | ...)
Slice or declarer	[....] (...)
Slice	**at** @
Identity relation	:= : **is**
Identity relation	:≠ : :/= : **isnt**
Dummy name	∘ **nil**
Jump	**goto**

Context	Alternatives
	go to
	(nothing)

Dummy unit	$\curvearrowright$
	skip

Comment	**comment** . . . **comment**
	co . . . **co**
	¢ . . . ¢
	# . . . #

Pragmat	**pragmat** . . . **pragmat**
	pr . . . **pr**

Appendix II
Summary of Constructs and Coercions

The following table shows the hierarchical classification of all constructs which are capable of standing on their own as phrases as well as forming parts of larger phrases. Subclassification is represented by indentation, so that, for example, a loop clause is a type of enclosed clause, which is a type of unit, but an enclosed clause is not a type of loop clause and a generator is not a type of formula. The table defines three terms not used in the text: a PRIMARY is any identifier, denotation, slice, call, cast, or enclosed clause; a SECONDARY is any selection, generator, or primary; and a TERTIARY is any formula, **nil** symbol, or secondary. A program consists of some enclosed clause, which may be labelled.

phrase
  declaration
    mode declaration
    identity declaration
    variable declaration
    operation declaration
    priority declaration
  unit (statement or expression)
    assignation
    identity relation
    jump
    skip
    routine text
    tertiary
      formula (monadic or dyadic)
      nil
      secondary
        selection
        generator
        primary
          identifier
          denotation (integer, real, Boolean, character, string, or bits)
          slice
          call
          cast
          format text
          enclosed clause
            closed clause

    loop clause
    parallel clause
    conditional clause
    case clause
    conformity clause
    collateral clause
      row display
      structure display
      collateral statement

Each position in a phrase occupied either by a series or by some type of unit is of a characteristic SORT, which specifies what coercions may be applied in determining the value of the construct. There are five different sorts of positions, called STRONG, FIRM, MEEK, WEAK, and SOFT positions. The applicable coercions are shown by the following table:

	strong	firm	meek	weak	soft
deproceduring	√	√	√	√	√
dereferencing	√	√	√	√	
uniting	√	√			
widening	√				
rowing	√				
voiding	√				

A weak position differs from a meek one in that if the construct corresponds to a name, it is never dereferenced to such an extent that the last **ref** is removed.

The next table is a simplified summary of the sort, the mode after the application of any coercions, and the most general type of construct for each position.

Position	Sort	Mode	Construct
After **if** or **elif**	meek	**bool**	series
After **case** or **ouse** in case clause	meek	**int**	series
After **then** or **else**	any	any	series
After **in** or , in case clause	any	any	unit
After **out** in case clause	any	any	series
After **for**	—	**int**	identifier
After **from, by,** or **to**	meek	**int**	unit
After **while**	meek	**bool**	series
After **do**	strong	**void**	series
After = in identity declaration	strong	non-**void**	unit
Before :=	soft	reference	tertiary (not **nil**)
After :=	strong	non-**void**	unit
One side of **is** or **isnt**	soft	reference	tertiary (not **nil**)
The other side of **is** or **isnt**	strong	reference	tertiary
After **of**	weak	(ref. to) structure	secondary
Before [	weak	(ref. to) multiple	primary
Subscript or bound	meek	**int**	unit

Position	Sort	Mode	Construct
After : in routine text	strong	any	unit
Operand	firm	non-**void**	formula or secondary
Before (in call	meek	procedure	primary
Actual parameter	strong	non-**void**	unit
After declarer in cast	strong	any	enclosed clause
Before; (if not a declaration)	strong	**void**	unit
Before **exit** or end of series	any	any	unit
Part of row or structure display	strong	non-**void**	unit
Part of collateral statement or parallel clause	strong	**void**	unit

This table does not account for the fact that the modes in many sets of related positions, such as the two sides of an assignation, are interdependent in some way. Also, balancing permits all but one of the value-yielding parts of a conditional clause, case clause, or series to be strong, regardless of the position of the construct as a whole.

Selected Bibliography

Except for those on Algol 68, these are illustrative references only. There are many other readily accessible books on the various topics.

General

A comprehensive, language-independent overview of most of the elementary concepts and applications of programming can be found in Forsythe *et al* (1975). Brown and Sampson (1973) discuss the methodology of designing and debugging practical programs. Some important concepts related to structured programming are discussed in Dahl *et al* (1972).

Algol 68

The official formal definition of the revised and final version of Algol 68, sponsored by International Federation of Information Processing, is to be found in van Wijngaarden *et al* (1974). The original language, which was rather more cumbersome to learn and to use, is defined in van Wijngaarden *et al* (1969); Peck (1972) is a companion volume to aid understanding of the latter report. Lindsey and van der Meulen (1971) give a less formal, much more entertaining, but still rather advanced and theoretical treatment of the original language. The most essential supplementary material for any reader of the present book is that which describes the peculiarities of the implementation(s) available to him.

Symbolic Processing and Commercial Applications

Text processing and other aspects of computational linguistics are described by Hays (1967). A good discussion of data structures and list processing can be found in Knuth (1969); Foster (1967) provides another introduction to list processing. The use of files in data processing is described by Judd (1973). Data processing is also the subject of Arnold *et al* (1972). Knuth (1973) presents a thorough compendium of algorithms for searching and sorting.

Numeric Applications

Fox and Mayers (1968) provide an introduction to numerical methods and numerical analysis. A more advanced treatment is given by Ralston (1965).

Arnold, R. R., H. C. Hill, and A. V. Nichols (1972), *Modern Data Processing*, Second edition, Wiley, New York.

Brown, A. R., and W. A. Sampson (1973), *Program Debugging*, Elsevier, Amsterdam.

Dahl, O-J., E. W. Dijkstra, and C. A. R. Hoare (1972), *Structured Programming*, Academic Press, London and New York.

Forsythe, A. I., T. A. Keenan, E. I. Organick, and W. Stenberg (1975), *Computer Science: A First Course*, Second edition, Wiley, New York.

Foster, J. M. (1967), *List Processing*, Macdonald, London.

Fox, L., and D. F. Mayers (1968), *Computing Methods for Scientists and Engineers*, Oxford University Press, London.

Hays, D. G. (1967), *Introduction to Computational Linguistics*, American Elsevier, New York.

Judd, D. R. (1973), *Use of Files*, American Elsevier, New York.

Knuth, D. E. (1969), *Fundamental Algorithms* (*The Art of Computer Programming*, *Volume 1*), Addison-Wesley, Reading, Mass.

Knuth, D. E. (1973), *Sorting and Searching* (*The Art of Computer Programming*, *Volume 3*), Addison-Wesley, Reading, Mass.

Lindsey, C. H., and S. G. van der Meulen (1971), *Informal Introduction to ALGOL 68*, North-Holland, Amsterdam.

Peck, J. E. L. (1972), *An ALGOL 68 Companion*, University of British Columbia Press, Vancouver.

Ralston, A. (1965), *A First Course in Numerical Analysis*, McGraw-Hill, New York.

van Wijngaarden, A., B. J. Mailloux, J. E. L. Peck, and C. H. A. Koster (1969), *Report on the Algorithmic Language ALGOL 68*, Mathematisch Centrum, Amsterdam.

van Wijngaarden, A., B. J. Mailloux, J. E. L. Peck, C. H. A. Koster, M. Sintzoff, C. H. Lindsey, L. G. L. T. Meertens, and R. G. Fisker (1974), *Revised Report on the Algorithmic Language ALGOL 68*, Supplement to ALGOL BULLETIN 36, Dept. of Computing Science, University of Alberta, Edmonton (Preliminary edition).

Index